**COMPLIMENTARY
EXAMINATION COPY**

Good News about Jesus
as told by Mark

COMPLIMENTARY
EXAMINATION COPY

# Good News about Jesus as told by Mark

by
THOMAS J. SMITH

ST. MARY'S COLLEGE PRESS
Christian Brothers Publications, Winona, Minnesota

To my parents,
Roy and Ceal,
whose Good News
about God, life, and love
was taught without a book.

Nihil Obstat: Reverend Anthony Farrell, PhD
Censor Deputatus
July 25, 1977
Imprimatur: †Gerald O'Keefe, D.D.
Bishop of Davenport
July 25, 1977

*Good News about Jesus as told by Mark* is an adaptation of *Jesus Alive! The Mighty Message of Mark* by the same author.

*Cover:*
THE WRITING OF THE DEAD SEA SCROLLS
from a serigraph
by Shraga Weil
Courtesy, Pucker/Safrai Gallery,
Boston
Safrai Gallery, Jerusalem

ISBN 0-88489-095-3
Library of Congress Catalog Card Number 77-89324
Copyright 1977 by St. Mary's College Press,
Winona, Minnesota 55987

# Contents

|       | Introduction | 7 |
|-------|---|---|
| ONE   | The Beginning | 11 |
| TWO   | Parables and Miracles | 25 |
| THREE | More than Bread | 41 |
| FOUR  | What Kind of Messiah? | 53 |
| FIVE  | Avoiding the Trap | 71 |
| SIX   | Death and Resurrection | 87 |

# Introduction

The truly good news about Jesus is that his saving action, his death and Resurrection, continues to affect us today. Reading about, praying over, and discussing this good news can be an experience of discovered or renewed faith. In many ways, faith in Jesus, in the reign of God, is a gift and a response to mystery. It is this gift, this mystery, that in the final analysis is the subject of this book.

The gospel of Mark is the focal point for our glimpse at the life, death, and Resurrection of Jesus. Mark was chosen because it is now considered the first gospel written, but this does not imply that Mark is more reliable than the other three accounts (Christians believe that all four gospels are the inspired Word of God). But Mark as the first written gospel is a likely place to begin. Besides, it seems that some of the other evangelists borrowed material from Mark's account. From another point of view, Mark's version was chosen for this book because it has the fewest references to Old Testament themes and passages. Many modern readers are not familiar with these references, and therefore Mark might be the easiest gospel to understand.

*Good News about Jesus as told by Mark* is an adaption of my previous book: *Jesus Alive: The Mighty Message of Mark*.

The content of the two books is basically the same. The original text was meant for high school or college classes. This present condensed version is offered primarily for adults who wish to read this book privately or who plan to read and discuss the material as part of a group experience in adult religious education. For example, a parish may offer a six-week program using this text as a basis for learning and discussion. Or an individual adult could invite a few friends to join him/her in forming a small discussion group using this book as their main source. Other possibilities might include a series of workshops on the gospels, a short course sponsored by a diocesan religious education office, or a part of an adult retreat program. Then, too, this book can be an opportunity for learning and inspiration to an adult who wishes to read it privately. Whatever the format, the hope is that this text will be an occasion for increased faith and greater knowledge.

Anyone using this book should read it together with the gospel of Mark. Before each chapter of *Good News about Jesus* there's a reference to a section in Mark's gospel. Read that section as well as the chapter in this book. A small Guide for Group Leaders is also available to anyone who is interested. This Guide contains some practical suggestions for adult discussion groups, some "answers" to the discussion questions at the end of each chapter in this book, and some background information on a few main themes in the gospel.

As you read the following pages, may you truly experience the good news of Jesus' continuing love for us.

# Good News about Jesus as told by Mark

**TWIN SOULS**
by Mirtala Bentov
Courtesy, Pucker/Safrai Gallery, Boston

"In those days Jesus came from Nazareth of Galilee and was baptized by John in the Jordan" Mark 1:9.

# ONE
# Mark 1:1-3:6

# The Beginning

### INTERPRETING THE TEXT

Mark writes his gospel backwards. He begins with his conclusion. The first thirteen verses are a prologue, an introduction which states his main theme. In a sense, the rest of his gospel is a repetition of these opening lines.

This evangelist calls his account of the life, death, and Resurrection of Jesus a gospel. The following 670 verses will be good news inviting the reader to rejoice. Mark then tries to explain *why* we should rejoice. Jesus is the Messiah and the Son of God, the one person the Jews had been waiting for all these years. At the end of the gospel, Jesus will be called "Son of God" again. There Mark puts those words in the mouth of a Roman centurion who was on guard duty at the foot of the cross. Just about everything between this first verse and that admission on Calvary is leading up to that centurion's proclamation. It's a true prologue: the writer states the conclusion, develops his story to explain what he means, and winds up with the same conclusion. During this process of development he hopes that the reader will agree with him by the time he gets to the end.

Since Mark is writing for Gentile readers, he avoids many

references to the Old Testament. But he couldn't avoid Old Testament ideas completely. In fact, it's impossible to eliminate all traces of Judaism from Jesus. As a result, Mark makes an immediate allusion to the Old Testament prophet, Isaiah. He wants to show in this prologue that John the Baptist had a special role to play; he was the forerunner of Jesus, the man who was supposed to prepare the people for Jesus.

John was a true prophet in the tradition of Jeremiah, Isaiah, Amos, and the others. He told the people to repent of their sins and change their lives. "Look out," he says, "you people are not living up to the faith. And you better get ready now, because someone is coming who's really going to put it to you." Those who accepted John's message were baptized in order to show publicly that they really did want to change their lives.

When Jesus appeared one day, he too wanted to receive John's baptism. The vision that Mark describes was seen only by Jesus, and it once again is full of Old Testament themes. The point here is that Jesus is the fulfillment of Jewish hopes, an idea that will receive further development as the gospel proceeds. The dove, which suggests the presence of the Spirit, was in the Old Testament a symbol of the whole nation of Israel, somewhat like the eagle is a symbol of the United States. Since the dove is present at the baptism of Jesus, the implication is that all of Israel is summed up in Jesus. Another aspect of this baptism account which could clarify the meaning of the passage is the reference to Jesus coming out of the water. This coming out or exodus is a reminder that Jesus repeats and improves upon the first exodus when the Jews crossed the Red Sea and escaped from the Egyptians. So once again Jesus fulfills the Old Testament and re-enacts within himself the history of the whole nation of Israel. But all of this is known only to the reader; it's a secret to the people of Jesus' time, since the vision, as Mark presents it, is seen exclusively by Jesus. According to Mark, the real identity of Jesus is kept secret until the centurion proclaims on Calvary that Jesus is the Son of God.

After his baptism, which begins Jesus' public ministry, he heads for the desert, the kind of place where the Jewish nation roamed twelve hundred years earlier, before they settled in Palestine. The number forty signifies a long time. There in the desert, Jesus is tempted. It's a battle between good and evil, and after considerable struggle, good wins out. This theme too—the conflict between good and evil—will recur over and over again in the rest of the gospel. Each time, just like here at the beginning, Jesus will triumph over the evil.

From chapter 1, verse 14, to chapter 3, verse 6, Mark builds on the themes he presented in the introduction. He's concerned about the reaction of the crowd to Jesus, the calling of some of his disciples (though they don't act like his disciples here), and the growing opposition of the Jewish leaders to Jesus. And in the background of all these themes is the main point: Jesus begins very cautiously to demonstrate who he is, his own identity. He comes to an awareness of his own identity, and he reveals that identity to the crowds gradually. He keeps his Messiahship a secret, mainly because the crowds wouldn't understand the kind of Messiah Jesus was. Mark develops his gospel in the same way, like a television mystery show which gradually unravels until the ending when everything becomes clear. We know then who did what and why. But until that time, it's a secret. The gospel of Mark deals with the "Messianic Secret."

If you want a two-line summary of what any gospel is about, just read Mark, chapter 1, verses 14 and 15: "After John's arrest, Jesus appeared in Galilee proclaiming the good news of God: 'This is the time of fulfillment. The reign of God is at hand! Reform your lives and believe in the gospel!'" This is an editorial faith-comment by Mark. The scene is Galilee, away from Jerusalem, where according to Mark, Jesus did most of his work. Mark's summary of the Jesus message is simple: "Through Jesus, God is among us. Believe that and live accordingly."

Notice there's no reference to the birth or infancy of Jesus in Mark's gospel. For Mark the important feature of Jesus is his proclamation of the reign of God, and that proclamation begins with his public ministry.

The next gospel episode recounted by Mark deals with discipleship. Jesus calls the "privileged" disciples first: Peter, James, and John. This is not just a passing casual meeting; it's an example of Jesus' power to create disciples. The impression here is that the disciples must give up their livelihood and abandon their families. But that's not really the point; rather, the idea is that discipleship entails great change. It's a question of priorities—what comes first. To be a disciple, a Christian must put the reign of God first, regardless of his job or family situation.

The rest of chapter 1 could be called a typical day in the ministry of Jesus. This section explains the authority of Jesus, both in word and deed. He teaches in the synagogue, and people are amazed. Mark doesn't tell us what he preaches, but as the gospel unfolds it becomes evident that the main message of Jesus is a declaration of who he is. It's a self-revelation—that's what he teaches in the first half of the gospel. And he does so in a veiled way. He taught in a way that was unusual, not like the scribes. He was not a "lower" teacher; he taught with power, the same power which overcame the evil forces in the temptation in the desert.

It's significant that the first miracle Mark recounts is an exorcism, that is, driving out a demon. Many miracles are described as exorcisms. Whether this means actual devil possession or whether it's a psychotic situation, isn't the real point. In either case, Jesus demonstrates his power over evil. The sickness, whatever its real nature, is a symbol of the power of destructive forces.

Jesus faces that power head-on and drives it away. He continues to meet those forces in many ways throughout the gospel. The final evil he deals with is his own death. And in that struggle, as in all the rest, he triumphs.

The gospel miracles, then, are very important to Jesus as he proclaims the arrival of the reign of God and to Mark as he records that proclamation. These miracles are signs that in and through Jesus the loving presence and power of God is, in a special way, made available to the world. They are another way of saying: "This is the time of fulfillment. The reign of God is at hand" (1:15).

The evil spirit recognizes Jesus as a force for good, but the crowd doesn't see it. The people are simply amazed by the curing and miss the message.

The story of Simon's mother-in-law provides some more insights into the message of Jesus. First of all, Peter had earlier left his trade to follow Jesus. But with this incident recounted almost immediately, we see that a disciple need not become indifferent to his family. Secondly, the setting here is the privacy of a home. The "privileged" disciples are there, and generally in those kinds of situations Jesus does something very special. The early Church viewed this episode as a preview of the coming Resurrection of Jesus, and that's the way Mark tells it. Thirdly, this story indicates another dimension of discipleship—namely, service of others. When Jesus makes a disciple, that person immediately serves others, as did Peter's mother-in-law. Finally, we know from this account that Peter was married, as is probably the case with all the disciples except John.

As his hectic day comes to an end, Jesus is imposed upon by other people. His day is a long one; he is probably tired, but he continues his work. Mark presents it this way to show that Jesus did not restrict his teaching and his concern to only a few chosen people. He helped all who came to him. Once again, the demons recognize Jesus as a source of good, even as the Messiah, but the crowds still don't get the message.

The crowds are excited by this spectacular healer. It's like a sideshow. That's why Jesus leaves that town (although Simon wants him to stay and capitalize on his growing popularity) and goes to the desert to pray. In Mark's gospel, when Jesus prays it is a time of great stress connected with the true nature of his Messiahship. The crowds aren't reacting the way he wanted; they see his power but don't hear his message. So Jesus leaves to think it all through and to pray about what he should do. He decides to move on to other places and try his luck there, the implication being that he was a little disappointed with this beginning of his ministry. Even Simon got it wrong.

The cure of a leper is significant because it indicates Jesus' power to save even those who were excluded from Israel by the law of Moses. Lepers were outcasts of society and could not participate in the social and religious life of Israel. Mark includes this cure in the story in order to demonstrate the extent of Jesus' ability to confront evil and surpass it. The man is sent back to the priest so that he can once again be accepted officially within Jewish society and religion. Typically he is asked to keep quiet about the cure—because Jesus is afraid the crowds would once again misinterpret the meaning of his power. The cured leper, of course, tells everyone about it. The early Church read this passage as an expression of their belief that those who are cleansed by Christ in baptism must "proclaim" the good news.

Most of chapter 2 deals with controversy. The Pharisees, a powerful group of Jewish religious and political leaders, are afraid of Jesus. They judge him to be unfit for teaching and to be misleading the people. Their attempts to trap Jesus in a violation of the Law take up a good part of the gospel. They are scandalized by Jesus' conduct and words.

The main message here is not difficult: Jesus claims the unusual power to forgive sins. The scribes and Pharisees object. Sin for them is a violation of the Law of Moses; and only God can forgive sinners, and then only if they meet the requirements of Law for forgiveness. Jesus shows them that the power he has in curing a paralysis, a sickness which is a symbol of the presence of evil, is the same power he has in curing sin, another kind of sickness and another sign of the presence of evil. Jesus' battle against evil is total—nothing escapes his desire to confront those destructive forces.

Characteristically, the people fail to see the miracle as a sign of Jesus' power to forgive sins. They marvel at the deed itself without understanding the meaning of the deed.

Mark follows immediately with another story that pits Jesus against the Pharisees. This time the topic is fasting, a practice the Pharisees are very insistent upon. Jesus is not opposed to fasting; he objects to the attitude which says that fasting automatically makes you a better person. Perhaps Jesus doesn't demand fasting of his followers because he wants to avoid the idea that fasting works automatically. Jesus looks for and encourages a personal faith response from people, not a particular practice. After that faith has been felt, then Christians can and should perform practices similar to fasting. But the faith commitment comes first, and during the life of Jesus that kind of faith response has not yet been made by the disciples.

The controversy with the Pharisees grows. Jesus now challenges them on a very sensitive topic: the observance of the Sabbath laws. The Pharisees were strict observers of all the many regulations regarding the Sabbath, and they felt that their salvation depended on keeping those laws exactly. Jesus responds to their accusation by playing their own legal game and beats them on their own ground. Even David violated the law when circumstances demanded it. Law is not unimportant, but faith is more important. The Sabbath is not unimportant, but man is more important. This attitude was helpful to the early Christians because they had to decide to what extent they would follow the Jewish Sabbath regulations.

Jesus goes back to the synagogue where the Pharisees are bound to see and hear him. He is not afraid of them. He cures a man with a withered hand—once again on the Sabbath. The time is what is important, not the cure. Mark records the anger of Jesus; the other evangelists seem embarrassed to do so.

In chapter 3, verse 6, we have the conclusion to this section of the gospel. The opposition Jesus meets from the Pharisees reaches its inevitable outcome: they plot to destroy him. The Pharisees join with the Herodians. That's a very unusual alignment, since those two groups oppose each other on everything else. Mark implies here that people of all kinds conspired to kill Jesus.

## SOME BACKGROUND NOTES

The gospel of Mark was probably the first one written. Most scholars believe that this account was compiled and written in Rome about the year 70. Some researchers think an earlier date of composition is also possible. The important thing is that it was not written right on the spot, as Jesus was experiencing the events. And since it was the first gospel, it seems that the other gospel writers, particularly Matthew and Luke, borrowed from Mark's account. They apparently had Mark's version in front of them as they composed their gospels.

But Mark didn't just sit down one day and start from scratch. He had materials in front of him too, written resources as well as the memories of eyewitnesses. Scripture scholars say that in the years between 30 and 50 there was a long written account of the Passion story (without the Resurrection appearances), and this account explains why the Passion passages in the four gospels are so similar (though there are differences too). Mark also used a number of collections of stories related to various aspects of Jesus' life. One seemed to contain a number of the miracle stories; another concentrated on the parables. In the process of writing the gospel Mark had to keep in mind the oral traditions of his Christian community as well as scattered written accounts.

Mark had at his disposal, then, both written and unwritten resources. He was a true author; he had a specific purpose, and he felt free to use his materials to develop that purpose. That's why some parables, for example, will basically be the same story in Matthew and Mark, and yet they will illustrate very different points.

It is good to recall as we read the gospels that we do not have a biography here. There would be many more details about Jesus' life if it were a biography. It's helpful to remember three levels of development of the gospels. The first level is the actual historical event. Something happened in Palestine in about the year 30 A.D., and what happened revolved around the life, death, and message of Jesus of Nazareth.

There is a second level which complicates our reading of the Scriptures. This is the level of the experiences the early Christian Church went through. In other words, by the time Mark wrote in 70 A.D., there were thirty-five or forty years of history to Christianity. The problems this primitive Christian Church had are reflected in the gospels. The gospels, in other words, tell us much about Jesus, but they tell us much about the first forty years of the Christian community as well. The difficulty arises in trying to determine when Mark is writing about Jesus directly and when he is writing about the early Church.

Then to complicate matters further, there's evidence of a

third level of experience reflected in the gospel, and that's the level of Mark himself. He adds his own interpretation to the events of Jesus' life and of the Church's life. He must rely on the written material he has before him and on the evidence provided by eyewitnesses, but he doesn't just copy that material. He forms it, pulls it together, and adds his own thoughts. He shapes it, using a style that is distinctively his own. He chooses the language. In brief, he puts his special stamp on the final product.

In understanding the gospel then, it's beneficial to know what level Mark is referring to: whether he's writing an historical account of the actual events in the life of Jesus, whether he's considering a problem the early Church is facing, or whether he's making an editorial comment, interpreting those events in his own way. Oftentimes, he might be referring to all three levels at the same time, or at least, within the same sentence. It makes reading the gospel more complicated, but it also opens the door to a greater richness of meaning when a person views the gospel from those three angles.

Where did the various gospels come from? Are they all the same? When are they different, and why? Why wasn't the early Church content with just one account? Did the gospel writers copy from each other? If so, how much copying went on? If they borrowed from each other, which one came first? And which gospel borrowed from which gospel?

Many theories have been advanced to explain the relationship among the synoptic gospels. Some people have suggested that prior to the writing of the gospels there was a common oral tradition in the early Church. This preaching took solid form almost immediately after the Resurrection and was repeated often. When the evangelists decided to write their gospels they each, independent of one another, drew on this early oral tradition. The differences in the gospels are due to the different styles of preaching.

Most modern critics would agree with this theory up to a point. They accept the importance of the oral tradition, but they conclude that oral tradition alone does not sufficiently explain the similarities among the three gospels; there must have been some literary exchange as well.

Many Scripture teachers believe that Mark came first but also that there were non-scriptural sources that Mark, Matthew, and Luke used in composing their gospels. These scholars say that enough evidence has been found to establish the existence of a document they call Q which has since been lost. Q would have been a collection of sayings by Jesus written in Greek. In this theory, Mark wrote his gospel first, but Matthew and Luke used both Mark and Q as their sources. This group of scholars seems to eliminate oral tradition, contending that the dependence of one gospel on another is due solely to common written sources. For that reason, this theory seems to be somewhat deficient.

Perhaps the most acceptable theory is one which would combine the elements of the other theories. This theory would accept the influence of oral tradition on the formation of all the gospels but also admit of a literary influence. This approach maintains that besides Q, there likewise existed various collections of hand-written materials about different aspects of the life of Jesus. For example, this theory speculates that there was a collection containing the parables of Jesus. This written document was available to all three writers, perhaps with some variations in form but with basically the same stories. Another written document available to all of them would be a Passion narrative. Mark is accepted as the oldest existent gospel, and Matthew and Luke are dependent on Mark. This multiple-document theory, including an oral tradition, is probably the best present explanation of the development of the gospels. We need to admit, however, that even this approach is not totally conclusive; the problem of the formation of the gospels has not been completely resolved. Perhaps it never will be.

The gospels are complicated masterpieces of literature. The record of Jesus' suffering and death is one example of that literary genius. And for the believer, these gospels are above all the word of God, a divine message shining through and working within the written message presented by the four evangelists.

A final word here about inspiration, that is, the Christian's belief that the Bible is the word of God. There have been volumes written, many theories proposed, and centuries-old discussions attempting to explain what inspiration really is and how it works. For our purposes, it is sufficient to say that if we can discover what the human author, in this case Mark, meant by what he wrote in his gospel, we can believe that God meant the same thing. Most theories about inspiration would accept that position. A big problem arises in discovering what the human author is saying; it's easy to miss the message. And if we miss his message we also miss God's message.

Inspiration implies a certain degree of faith. Without that faith, the gospels may be interesting testimonies to the life and death of Jesus of Nazareth, but they can never be what the authors intended them to be. Mark was writing to and for believing Christians; it is an account flowing from his faith in the divinity of Jesus and the importance of the Christian message. That faith leaps out at the reader from the pages of the gospel. But it's a faith that cannot be forced; the reader will have to face the questions himself and answer them himself. What do you think of Jesus of Nazareth? Who is he? What does he want of us? Mark has answered those questions, and he wants to share those answers with us. He hopes that we will agree with him.

## DISCUSSION TOPICS

1) *Jesus accepted the baptism of John (1:9-11). With this event, Jesus began his public ministry. Keeping this in mind, discuss the following situation. The Jacksons and the Hamiltons have been friends a long time, and they share many interests: they vacation at the same Michigan fishing resort, they attend the same political caucuses, they have about the same income, and they even prefer the same restaurants when they dine out. The Jacksons are baptized church-goers, however, and the Hamiltons are not. Should there be some basic differences in the life styles of these two couples in view of the fact that the Jacksons are participating church members? Explain your answer.*

2) *The brief account of the temptation in the desert (1:12-13) raises the whole issue of the relationship between good and evil. Suppose that a friend of yours becomes depressed because of the evil in the world, such as war, poverty, hatred, etc. What would you say to your friend if he/she talked to you about this depression?*

3) *The sinners and tax collectors were considered outcasts in Jesus' society, and yet he associated with these people (2:13-17). In our society a similar situation exists. For example, the Wilsons live in an area that will probably become a racially mixed neighborhood in a short time. If you were the Wilsons, how would you react to this situation? What would you say to your neighbors? to your children?*

4) *Jesus insists on the need to change, to renew ourselves, to seek conversion (1:16-20). When and how much do we need to change? Some people accept and welcome most changes; others resist almost any change. How do you rate yourself in regard to change? How do you feel about such controversial issues as the changing role of women, increasing automation, foreign aid, changes in your church?*

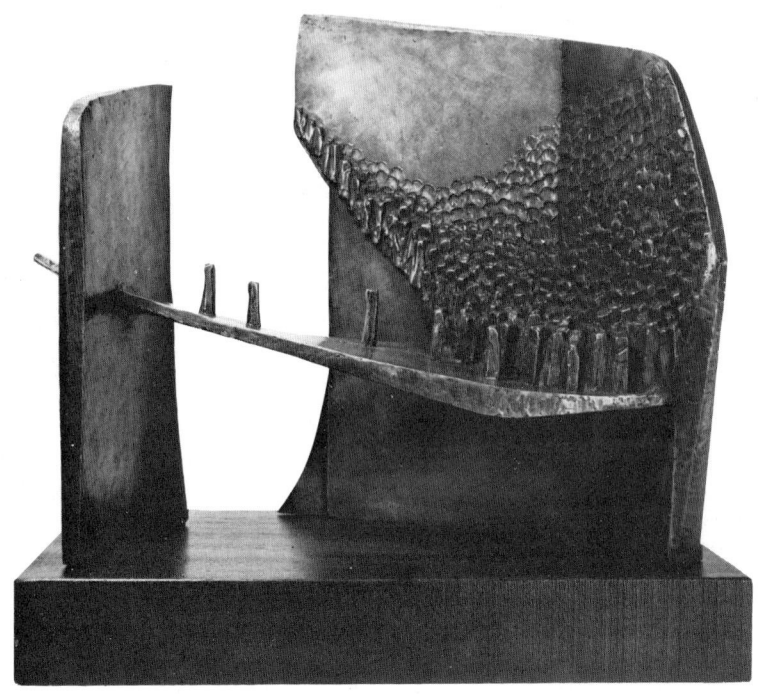

### THE ONLY BRIDGE
by Mirtala Bentov
Courtesy, Pucker/Safrai Gallery, Boston

"Jesus withdrew with his disciples to the sea, and a great multitude from Galilee followed . . . " Mark 3:7.

# TWO
## Mark 3:7-6:6

# Parables and Miracles

### INTERPRETING THE TEXT

The disappointing reaction of the crowd to his preaching and healing leads Jesus into phase two of his ministry. He decides to concentrate on forming a small group of special disciples, the hope being that with an intense training period and personal relationship with Jesus, they will finally understand his message.

In forming his small group of twelve, Jesus indicates his close connection with the Old Testament. The twelve apostles are a symbolic continuation of the twelve tribes of Israel. These select disciples are to be close to Jesus, to be his companions. A mark of apostleship then is this closeness to the Master; and in the early Church, after the Resurrection, it is precisely this constant companionship which provided the apostles with the base of their influence. St. Paul has to go to some length to prove his apostleship, because he did not experience this closeness in the same way the twelve did. It is obvious from the text that Jesus wanted this group to be "special." They even receive power to drive out demons, that is, they participate in establishing the reign of God in a very dramatic way.

The names of the twelve are interesting, and the listing is

probably included here to demonstrate the diversity within the group. Jesus did not pick all the same kind of people; they were from different economic and social backgrounds (Peter the fisherman, Matthew the tax-collector). Simon the Zealot was undoubtedly a political activist; the Zealot party was dedicated to the overthrow of the Romans, with violence if necessary. It's not surprising that the gospels give indications that this group didn't get along together too well. They argued among themselves about who was the best, and they disputed with Jesus and each other about the methods of preaching and what they should do next. The fact that Judas eventually betrayed Jesus indicates that this "disciple" could be disloyal not only to the Master but also to the other eleven men. The force of Jesus' personality must have been powerful in order to hold that group together as he did.

The opposition to Jesus continues, and it seems to expand. Even his kinsmen join in condemning him. They conclude that he is insane, while the scribes claim that he is possessed by the devil. Both those accusations amount to the same thing, since insanity in those days was considered the work of the devil. It's to be expected therefore that Jesus would begin to feel lonely and disappointed; even his family participated in the opposition which eventually led to his death.

The response Jesus makes once again confounds his accusers. "How in the world can I be working for the devil, when I'm driving out devils? If you're going to condemn me for something, you're going to have to come up with something better than that!"

Mark then includes the passage about the true family of Jesus, possibly because a few verses earlier, his blood relatives called him insane. The "brothers and sisters" of Jesus can easily be understood as his cousins, since that's one of the meanings of the original word. This episode does not indicate a lack of tenderness for relatives; it merely reminds us that the bond of brotherhood in the reign of God is greater than blood ties. At times discipleship makes demands which go farther than the demands even of a natural family.

Chapter 4 of Mark's gospel is confusing. Most of this section consists of a number of parables. But that's not the most confusing part; the problem comes in when we try to separate one parable from another. The three levels of the development of a gospel are very much in evidence in this passage: the first level of the earliest tradition, when the three parables were simply combined; the second level of the explanation of the parable of the sower which a later church community probably used in instruction classes; and, finally, the third level of Mark's personal comments, which can be discerned particularly in verses 11 and 12.

Summarized, these 34 verses include the following: three parables, two sayings, the interpretation of a parable, a saying about the purpose of parables, an introduction, and a conclusion.

More than likely these parables came late in Jesus' public career. Mark uses them rather early in his gospel, because they deal with the nature of the reign of God in a veiled way.

Jesus never actually gives us a scientific definition of the reign of God, simply because such a definition is impossible. At the center of the reign of God lies mystery, and mystery, of its nature, cannot be captured in words. How and why God mingles with us are questions that are ultimately unanswerable. But this mystery can be hinted at, pointed to, symbolized, and partially expressed. The parables are one way in which Jesus proclaims the presence of the reign of God. He does not define the reign of God, but he does tell us what it is like and what it is not like. The parables thus play an important part in this teaching.

The stories are meant to encourage Jesus' followers; the reign is here, but it's going to take some time for it to be completed. The disciples are expecting Jesus to take over the world, but he runs into opposition. They need to be patient amid all the adversity. In the early Church many Christians expected the second coming of Jesus within the near future, but the second coming did not happen; so *they* needed the message of patience as well. The parables give assurance: despite all the setbacks and delay in the final victory over the forces of evil, the reign is truly established.

The contrast in the parable of the sower is between the three types of unfruitful soil and the good soil in which the seed grows. The lesson is obvious: the reign of God will surely come even though it may not appear so. We must wait for the seed in the fruitful soil to grow. But its eventual fruitfulness is guaranteed.

Mark then states very clearly that some people will not understand the parables, not because the stories themselves are difficult but because some people don't want to hear the message. Or perhaps they can't understand it since their concept of the Messiah was so much different from Jesus' concept. In any case, the implication here is that a person who has faith will appreciate the richness of the parables, while an unbeliever will not.

The interpretation of the parable of the sower in verses 13-20 is probably the result of religious instructions given by members of the early Christian Church. The style of language and the vocabulary lead us to this conclusion. For example, the term *the word*, which appears eight times in this short section, was a technical phrase used by the early Church for the gospel message. Besides, this interpretation concentrates on the different types of unfruitful soil, but this wasn't the main point of the original parable. It seems that this expansion of the sower story is geared towards encouraging perseverance in times of temptation and persecution.

The parable of the seed is similar to the story of the sower. Here the emphasis is on the inactivity of the farmer after he sows the seed. Once planted in good soil the seed will grow and the harvest will come. In other words, the fulfillment of the reign of God will surely come, since Jesus has already planted the seed.

Mark immediately adds a third parable related to planting. This time the reference is to the mustard seed. This seed is called the smallest of all the seeds, yet it really isn't the smallest. But the size of the seed isn't the real point. The main idea is to draw a contrast between seemingly insignificant beginnings and the final outcome: what starts small will grow to amazing proportions. The good news from Jesus will spread throughout the world until it reaches fulfillment. This one person living in this tiny land ushers in a worldwide revolution.

The conclusion of this section on parables re-emphasizes the intention and the results of Jesus' use of parables. Mark reminds us again that the crowds didn't understand Jesus, even when he tried to spell it out in simple story form. Consequently, Jesus was forced to turn more and more to his disciples, hoping that with his fuller explanations they at least would know what he was saying.

Mark follows his presentation of three parables with an account containing three miracles, each performed for the benefit of the disciples. The crowds are still in the picture, but they continue to take a secondary place. A few chapters later in the gospel they will disappear almost completely, only to reappear during the Passion.

The first miracle is generally considered to be a personal recollection of the apostle Peter. But the episode is so reworked by the early Church that it is almost impossible to separate the actual event from the interpretation of the event by that community. The Church turned to this miracle for consolation because the term *boat* has long been a symbol of the Church. There's a strong emphasis here on the storm and the need for faith, and so this incident becomes a lesson in discipleship under stress.

In this miracle Jesus is called "Master" or "Teacher." Throughout the gospel of Mark this title is used in catechetical settings, episodes used by the first century Church to explain various aspects of Christianity. Employed here, it helps establish the fact that this miracle account was developed and reorganized to fit the purposes of the early Church.

Jesus condemns the disciples for their lack of faith. This judgment seems to be quite strong if we take it literally; that is, if Jesus made that condemnation before his Resurrection. More likely this judgment comes from Mark himself, as he remembers the disciples' loss of faith at Jesus' death.

The second miracle is hard to explain because of the connection between the swine and the maniac. One possible interpretation of this aspect of the story is that evil is self-destructive; that is, left to itself evil will destroy itself. Evil needs to fight against good, needs a foothold in good. Without that foothold, evil can't exist.

What may be even more significant than the miracle itself is its location, where it takes place. The territory of the Gerasene is outside of Israel. The maniac is a Gentile, and according to acceptable social customs among the Jews of Jesus' time, association with Gentiles was strongly discouraged. Jesus confronted the power of the demons and defeated evil again, this time the result being an interest in Jesus by people outside Judaism. This theme of concern for Gentiles was certainly consoling for those Christians who were not Jewish.

Jesus does not allow the cured man to accompany him. It's hard to say why, but the important aspect of this part of the story is that Jesus does not appeal to the Messianic Secret. Rather he tells the man to proclaim what has happened to him. Perhaps this command is due to the fact that the man is not a Jew and therefore does not entertain any false expectations of the coming Mes-

## Parables and Miracles / 31

siah. He can therefore simply proclaim what has happened and not draw any erroneous conclusions.

The third miracle is actually a combination of two different stories. The one concerns the daughter of Jairus, an influential man from the Jewish synagogue; and the second revolves around the woman suffering from a hemorrhage. Mark combines them, probably because of their similarity.

The confidence that Jairus exhibits is a distinct contrast to the distrust and hostility of the scribes. He expresses his belief that Jesus can do something for his daughter, and whenever Jesus meets that kind of faith he offers to help. But the main purpose for including this episode in the gospel is to make a commentary on death. The raising of the daughter is a preview of Jesus' own resurrection; this is a key miracle for Mark, because miracles symbolize the passage from death to life. In this story Jesus confronts death directly and overcomes it; death is considered a major result of the forces of evil. Jesus does battle with evil in many ways, but none so directly as when he faces death, his own or others'.

The woman with the hemorrhage suffers not only because a physical ailment has caused her many years of affliction, but also because she is considered "unclean" according to Jewish ceremonial law. To say the least, it was a grave inconvenience to her. It almost seems that the power of Jesus works like magic in this instance, but Mark immediately corrects that possible interpretation by the woman's admission of her "touching" his cloak. Jesus then says very clearly that her faith was a necessary disposition for the cure to take place. Touching Jesus generally means more than a physical contact; it likewise implies a touching of the person or the spirit of Jesus.

This section of the gospel closes with another and more extensive account of the rejection of Jesus. Previously, in chapter

3, verse 6, the Pharisees and the Herodians began to plot against him. Here Jesus is condemned by his townspeople. While his popularity spreads, he likewise gains more enemies. Nazareth is the presumed place of this rejection, but in the context of the whole gospel this negative reaction is a foreshadowing of the final rejection in which all the people concur. It's interesting to note that Jesus teaches in Nazareth, but the crowd's response here is almost the exact opposite of their response in chapter 1, verses 21-27. There he found enthusiasm; here he runs into skepticism leading to explicit disbelief. These people want to know, "Who is this man?" It's a good question, the basic question in terms of Mark's gospel. This group, however, does not ask the question honestly; they ask it in order to put Jesus down since they resent him. Because their attitude was so cynical and unbelieving, he could work no miracle there. This verse provides us with a clear example of the necessity for faith before Jesus can help an individual. Mark adds immediately, however, that not all the people rejected Jesus, and he could help those who accepted him.

This incident brings to a tragic end his ministry in Galilee and previews his complete rejection by the whole nation. After this episode, Jesus is determined more than ever to concentrate his efforts on the select twelve disciples; they begin to take a more active role in proclaiming the presence of the reign of God.

## SOME BACKGROUND NOTES

Jesus used parables to help proclaim his message. As effective teaching devices, the parables referred to life situations familiar to his audience. But a parable is not an allegory. Both figures of speech involve the telling of a story, although there are important differences between the two.

First, what is a parable? The word *parable* comes from the

Greek, and it means the "placing of things side by side for the sake of comparison." In a parable a story is told, and although the story may be fiction, it is still true to life. This feature, this true-to-lifeness, distinguishes a parable from a fable.

Then what is an allegory? In an allegory, each detail and character of the story is significant, oftentimes having a hidden meaning. Allegories tend to portray abstract truth.

The important thing to remember about the distinction between an allegory and a parable is this: in a parable the most significant idea is the lesson of the whole story; the details serve only to bring out the main point. In an allegory, however, all the aspects of the story and each detail have an important meaning. Sometimes, in a story which is basically a parable, there may be some allegorical features. In other words, in a story with one main point (parable) some of the characters or details may have a significance of their own (allegory).

This distinction is needed because Jesus told stories. If these stories are parables, we have to interpret them one way; if they are allegories, we have to interpret them differently, trying to discover the meaning of each detail.

Most Scripture scholars today would say that the stories of Jesus are basically parables, with some allegorical features mixed in occasionally. In chapter 4 of Mark's gospel we read the parable of the sower. In verses 1-9, we find an example of a true parable, a story that has one main point. But in verses 13-20, we discover what appears to be an allegorical interpretation of the original story. More than likely, this allegorical interpretation was developed by the primitive Christian Church and not by Jesus himself.

Jesus was a good teacher, and this is seen in his use of parables. His illustrations were from daily life and they caught the attention of his listeners. At times he tossed in an unusual ending, a novel twist, that challenged his listeners to reflect on the main point. An example is the story of the woman who finds one small coin and rejoices exceedingly, over-rejoices it seems, just because she found one little coin. That technique was used to make people think.

The parables of Jesus are not just cute, clever stories to inspire people. Many of them express his main purpose; namely, to proclaim the presence of the reign of God. As such, they are an integral part of his mission and imply a vigorous assault made by God against the forces of evil. The parables in chapter 4 of Mark's gospel were an explanation and an apology for the slowness and "insignificant" results of Jesus' own ministry in Galilee. And yet, they describe the reality of Jesus' power and give assurance of his final, complete victory.

To understand the gospel of Mark, we also have to consider the question of miracles. To eliminate the miracle stories or to relegate them to fantasyland, to an area of relative unimportance, would be to cut a large portion out of the gospel. Those accounts are there—all over the place. They demand some kind of response.

One of the problems related to biblical miracles is that we have gradually learned to take them out of context. We have isolated the accounts of miracles, using them as weapons in our arguments to prove the divinity of Jesus. This approach is unfortunate, not because it is false in itself, but because it emphasizes an aspect of miracles which is not primary in the Scriptures. The gospels take the miraculous for granted; they do not try to prove the possibility of miracles. The gospels are concerned with *how* Jesus used miracles and what they meant to the evangelist.

In clarifying these two differing approaches, it is helpful to turn to a definition of miracles as formulated by St. Thomas Aquinas, who said that a miracle is an "action which surpasses the power of all nature." That formulation, or a similar one, is the generally accepted description of a miracle; it's an action which goes beyond the laws of nature.

Without quarreling with that definition, it is legitimate to point out that the biblical writers thought of miracles in very different terms. The Bible does not view nature as a closed system of laws; a clear distinction between natural and supernatural cannot be found in Scripture. Rather the "natural" and the "supernatural" are so joined together, are so blurred, that a separation of the two becomes impossible and artificial. According to the Bible, the workings of nature, of normal events (like a flood or an invasion by an enemy army), are attributed directly to God. In other words, sometimes the Bible includes as equally miraculous those acts which can be explained on the natural level. Therefore, the Bible includes events which St. Thomas could not accept as miraculous, even though Scripture unashamedly refers to them as miracles.

It might be helpful also to point out that the word *miracle* does not actually appear in the New Testament. The English translation may be a little misleading here. The English word *miracle* comes from the Latin word *miraculum*, which means "something to be wondered at." But the gospels were not written originally in Latin; they were written in Greek and Hebrew, with Aramaic having a very strong influence as well. The significance of this language reminder is that translations from one language to another sometimes lose the flavor of the original. In the case of the word *miracle*, which in English denotes an element of the marvelous, we find the biblical text referring not to the marvelous aspect but rather to the aspect of sign. Put another way, we discover that the scriptural reference to what we translate as miracle means in the original Hebrew or Greek a symbolic sign or an act of power. The Bible therefore does not give real emphasis to the marvelous character of a miracle; in fact, it need not refer to anything marvelous. Miracle in the biblical sense refers to any action or event which is a sign of God's presence, or any act of power reflecting that presence.

These reflections are not just playing with words; they are distinctions needed in order to understand what Mark meant when he wrote about the miracles of Jesus. We make a mistake when we use our definition of miracle as spelled out by St. Thomas Aquinas and assume that the word meant exactly the same thing for Mark. To summarize the difference, and perhaps run the risk of oversimplifying, we might say that the common understanding of miracle (as with St. Thomas) means an exceptionally marvelous happening, whereas for Mark it meant a symbolic act. Those two descriptions are not absolutely opposed, but they do express a different approach.

A safe conclusion would be that the miracles as recorded in the gospel of Mark are of secondary importance to the message of Mark. It's the message and the mission of Jesus which is the primary theme and most emphatic aspect of the gospel. The miracles are part of that message and factors in that mission, but they do not stand alone. In a sense, they are visual aids used by Jesus and probably expanded by the early Church and Mark, used in order to help explain the main thrust of the message of Jesus. They are symbolic acts which tell of the arrival of the reign of God. They say that God's reign has already begun, here and now, that God working through Jesus is stronger than Satan. As such, the miracles are not just added on to prove the importance of the message; they are rather an integral part of the revelation since they demonstrate the power of Jesus' actions. They are a vehicle of the message, and they are a weapon in Jesus' struggle with the forces of evil. To eliminate the miracles from the gospels would be to eliminate a necessary part of the basic message of Jesus. Mark couldn't tell the complete story without them. Neither can we.

## DISCUSSION TOPICS

*1) As a family the Harters are practicing Christians. Jane, the oldest daughter, is a college freshman. Home from school for Christmas vacation, she says in a family discussion that she now finds it hard to believe in Jesus because he lived so long ago. She claims that the apostles who saw and heard Jesus daily (3:13-19) had an advantage over us. "Besides," she says, "the twentieth century is so much more advanced than Jesus' times, and people today so much more educated that the message of Jesus doesn't apply any more." As a parent, how would you respond to a daughter who talked like this?*

*2) The gospel explanation of the parable of the sower (4:13-20) has many applications. One approach is to interpret the three kinds of bad seed as examples of obstacles that can prevent the growth of faith. The following case illustrates this interpretation. A friend of your son has become interested in Hinduism. He maintains that the world today presents great obstacles to being truly religious and that the only solution is to renounce the world completely. "Discover God by turning into yourself and away from all distractions as much as possible," he says. How would you respond to this advice?*

*3) At a party the conversation turns to religion. One person strongly criticizes and condemns religion as superstitious, outmoded, and even harmful. Would you publicly express your religious convictions in this kind of situation? Would you do so in any kind of situation? Doesn't Jesus command us to speak out (4:21-23)?*

*4) One of your high school daughter's best friends is a girl who has a reputation for being a troublemaker and "a little strange." You have heard from usually reliable people that this girl's ideas and values are "different," that she was suspended from school for being disrespectful to a teacher, and that she was recently fired from a part-time job. You don't like the way she dresses, but she has always been friendly to you. What would be your view of the friendship your daughter has with this girl? Would you talk to your daughter about the girl? What would you say? Would you talk to the girl about her reputation? What would you say? Do you see a connection between this situation and the condemnations (3:20-22) that Jesus also faced? Explain.*

**COURAGE OF FULL VISION**
by Mirtala Bentov
Courtesy, Pucker/Safrai Gallery, Boston

"And he called to him the twelve, and began to send them out two by two, and gave them authority over the unclean spirits" Mark 6:7.

# THREE
## Mark 6:7-7:37

# More than Bread

### INTERPRETING THE TEXT

Here begins a decisive new direction in the ministry of Jesus. According to Mark, he has been trying for some time to get away from the crowds, not because he has completely lost his popularity (even though his townspeople have just rejected him) but because the crowds continue to misinterpret his message about who he is. At this point in the gospel, Jesus succeeds in his desire to concentrate on instructing the disciples. This passage begins with the mission of the twelve, is interrupted by the report of the beheading of John the Baptist, and then proceeds to the recounting of the multiplication of the loaves, with its numerous sequels.

By comparison with Matthew's gospel, Mark's rendition of the mission of the twelve is brief, and it seems to be a preparation for Jesus' future self-revelation as the Messiah. Characteristically, Mark omits an instruction found in Matthew; that is, according to Matthew the disciples are not to go to the Gentiles. But since Mark is writing for Gentile readers, he skips that little detail. Likewise, in Luke's gospel the command to the disciples is to preach the coming of the reign of God. But here in Mark the disciples are to preach repentance for sin. Mark reserves the proclamation of the reign of God to Jesus himself; therefore, the disciples are to be like John the Baptist, that is, to awaken the people to the fact that someone else (Jesus) is coming to proclaim the reign. The differences in these accounts may seem subtle, but the point is that these differences reflect various theological approaches used by the gospel writers. They are not all saying exactly the same thing, and we shouldn't expect that they would.

The rather detailed account of John's death is staged in three scenes. The first scene describes the accusation John made to Herod. The gospel maintains that Herod imprisoned John because the prophet denounced Herod's adultery. But it may also be true that Herod feared John because of John's disciples and his influence on the people. If this political motive was part of the intrigue, we have a picture of the shaky security Herod felt as a puppet of the Romans. Scene two depicts Herodias tricking her husband into beheading John. The third scene foreshadows the burial of Jesus. In other words, Mark develops parallels between John and Jesus, particularly in the fact that John, like Jesus, was killed for his preaching.

The narrative resumes then with the return of the apostles from their mission. This is the only place in the gospel where Mark calls them apostles; he ordinarily refers to them as disciples, but, since he just mentioned John's disciples, he probably uses the title *apostle* here to distinguish Jesus' followers from John's followers. Here *apostle* means "those sent out."

The passage known as the Loaves Section includes everything from chapter 6, verse 31, to chapter 8, verse 26. Two accounts of the multiplication of bread highlight this unit, and each bread episode is followed by incidents recalling the feeding of the people.

Whenever Jesus wants to be alone with his disciples he is preparing them for a special revelation about himself. In Mark's view then, the feeding of the five thousand was performed primarily for the sake of the twelve. Jesus suggests that they rest for a while, probably because they are tired from their mission work.

The rest period also adds an Old Testament dimension to the scene, particularly implying a shepherd theme. Jesus is like the good shepherd who gives his flock a rest. This shepherd theme continues throughout the passage, with overtones of the shepherd as the Messiah providing a messianic banquet for his people. Jesus wants to bring God's word (food) to a hungry people. An obvious Old Testament reference in this account is the story of the Israelites surviving on manna in the desert after they escaped from the Egyptians.

The actual multiplying of the loaves has been expanded by the early Church by adding details from the words used at the Eucharist. The twelve baskets of leftovers are a sign of God's fullness; there is enough for all, to feed all the people in the New Israel. Surprisingly, there is no remark about the crowd being amazed, as is the usual response to a Jesus miracle. The lack of this detail suggests that this multiplication episode is a sign to the twelve Apostles disclosing the secret of Jesus' identity as the Messiah.

The gospels of Matthew, Mark, and Luke all include the miracle of Jesus walking on the water immediately after the multiplication of the loaves. The connection between the two incidents becomes more obvious when we place them side by side, one commenting on the other. Walking on the water is interpreted by the Apostles as a sign of the Messiah, just as feeding the five thousand is a sign of the messianic banquet. The description of the water scene indicates that this episode is especially designed to elicit a faith response, faith in Jesus as the Messiah. But Mark's conclusion states very clearly that the disciples still don't understand who Jesus is, even after the multiplication of the loaves and the walking on water. If they had really understood the message of the loaves, they would have known who it was coming to them on the water. Mark continually points out the disciples' inability to perceive the meaning of Jesus.

The popularity of Jesus reaches its high point after the feeding of the people in the desert. They recognize him everywhere and bring him the sick. He cures them, but Mark is not very enthusiastic in the way he presents these cures. He simply mentions them, in a tone that seems weary.

Jesus has just performed two dramatic signs of his identity as the Messiah. Now Mark introduces the Pharisees again, in order to demonstrate some of the differences between the teachings of the Jewish leaders and the teachings of Jesus' messianic reign. The conflict here focuses on the unwritten laws of the Pharisees, laws which they observed with the same dedication as the written laws of Moses. Jesus insists on a distinction between these two kinds of regulations. He is in opposition to the legalism of the Pharisees.

In verse 2 the reference to the disciples' eating habits is a link to the previous account of the feeding of the five thousand. Mark then adds a rather detailed explanation of these eating customs of the Jews, an explanation that would not be necessary if the readers were Jews themselves. The Pharisees are exposed as hypocrites in their worship because they follow the regulations of man even when these rules contradict the commands of God. Jesus then gives an example of what he means. He refers to the practice of Corban, the procedure of making a gift to God. Apparently, what some of the Pharisees were doing was offering their money as a gift to God. As a result they couldn't give it to anyone else, but they could use it themselves. They were using this practice of Corban as an excuse for not helping their fathers and mothers, even though there was no old age pension or social security in Jewish society. If the older parents were not cared for by their family, there was no one to do it. They were poverty-stricken and neglected. The Pharisees were obviously violating the command of God to care for their parents, and doing so under a legal cover.

*More than Bread* / 45

Besides, they were probably bragging about their devotion in giving their money to God. Jesus' condemnation of them is strong and uncompromising.

The next section is quite clear in its insistence on man's evil coming from within himself, not from outside. In effect, Jesus internalizes the whole question of what constitutes sin. This passage is also significant in terms of the development of the gospel. Once again the disciples are alone with him, and Jesus uses the opportunity to inform them that in the new reign of God there will be a necessary reversal of values: a man will be responsible for the actions he himself initiates.

According to Mark, Jesus now switches his locality. He heads for the territory of the Gentiles, and the setting is provided for the primary message in this section: Jesus is Messiah not only for the Jews but for all men. Jesus is recognized again; the repeated mention of this recognition is building to a time when he will be recognized as the Messiah. At first Jesus refuses to help the Syro-Phoenician woman, perhaps in order to emphasize his unsuccessful attempt to convince Israel of his mission. They had a chance, more than any other nation, more than this Gentile woman. In any case, Jesus does help the woman; he is Messiah to the Gentiles as well.

The account which follows, the healing of the deaf-mute, has much the same lesson. It also reflects a Gentile setting and repeats the command to maintain the Messianic Secret. The reaction of the crowd is unusually strong; they "proclaim" what they have seen and proclamation is a Christian term for the good news about Jesus. The reference to Jesus' doing everything well may be an allusion to the first book of the Bible, implying that Jesus has initiated a new creation.

## SOME BACKGROUND NOTES

Most of the words and actions of Jesus flowed from his desire to establish firmly the reign of God and to have that reign recognized and accepted by his followers. At least that's the way Matthew, Mark, and Luke present their gospels. John's gospel approaches the meaning of the life of Jesus from a different perspective. His view is more "poetic."

Mark makes use of the phrase *the reign of God* frequently. This phrase summarizes the core of Jesus' preaching, and as such it is a key concept in understanding the gospel. The Messiah announces the new reign of God. Since the concept of the Messiah as popularly held by the crowds was considerably different from, if not opposed to, Jesus' view of the Messiah, it's not surprising that there would be significant variations between Jesus and the crowds about the nature of the reign of God as well.

There is no doubt that Jesus used the term *the reign of God* in his preaching. Mark's gospel alone mentions that phrase fourteen times, most of the time in very crucial passages. Jesus proclaims this reign from the beginning of his public ministry, indicating that he saw himself in a unique position, as the one who was to announce and usher in this new reign. He was a breakaway from the age of the Old Testament; his mission was distinctive, he changed things radically. And yet he did not wipe out the Old Testament tradition; he did not destroy it. He claimed to fulfill it and to begin on a new plateau. In some mysterious way the heavenly reality of God descended into human history and became particularly present in Jesus of Nazareth. Full participation in this reign is reserved for heaven or to the end of the world when all things will be completed according to the power and designs of God. But the reign is a reality now as well. It is here, but it is not yet fully recognized or completely extended.

For the prophets of the Old Testament and for Jesus, the

reign of God would express the will of God for the nation of Israel. By the time of Jesus the people had switched it around; for them the reign of God meant that Yahweh would do the will of the people. The people, specifically the Jewish religious and political leaders, would determine what *they* wanted, and Yahweh became the means by which their purposes would be fulfilled. They wanted to control God. It's in this context that Jesus opposes and attacks the Pharisees. A good example of this conflict is found in chapter 7 of Mark's gospel.

Another important aspect of the reign of God as preached by Jesus is the call to repentance, to forgiveness. But the Jewish leaders don't know what to be sorry for. Repent of what? They follow the law; they go to the temple and to the synagogue. They feel therefore that they have a good relationship with God. In effect, Jesus is saying that the law is not a sure guide for salvation; it does not contain a complete statement about the will of God. More is demanded. The security felt by the Pharisees is a false security, and their holier-than-thou attitude is to be condemned. They too, as well as everyone else, must seek forgiveness, admitting that they at times can hurt their neighbors and thereby bring evil into the world. It's precisely this call for repentance that Jesus insists upon in his confrontation with the Pharisees regarding the practice of Corban. But they stubbornly refuse to admit their need for forgiveness, and for this reason the Pharisees cannot participate in the new reign of God.

The reign of God is a term which includes and summarizes just about the whole of Jesus' preaching. As such, it has many aspects to it. In the stories about the multiplication of the loaves and the walking on the water, Jesus is trying through these events to announce that the reign of God is here in him, the Messiah. From the beginning of his gospel to its final verse, Mark is describing this reign, pointing to Jesus as the Messiah who brings it about, and inviting his readers to adopt those qualities of life which are in conformity with membership in that reign. We can read each episode of the gospel with this question in mind: what does this incident have to say about Jesus and the reign of God? Properly understood, it will say something about it.

It might seem strange that Jesus was constantly telling people, especially those he just cured, to keep quiet about the cure. Mark emphasizes this aspect of the gospel. But both Mark and Jesus had a very good reason for presenting the message this way.

Jesus lived at a particular time, in a particular place. What the people at that time and place felt and thought was extremely important. The message Jesus wanted to deliver had to be offered in a language the people could understand. Jesus had to speak their language. And words have different meanings; sometimes the same word has different meanings for different people. Take the word *freedom*, for example. For some people, freedom means doing whatever they want when they want to do it; for others, it means consideration of others and their needs; and for still others, it implies the making and the enforcing of good laws. Then there's the distinction between political freedom, social freedom, economic freedom, and personal, psychological freedom. Discussions on freedom can be confusing when it isn't clear what kind of freedom individuals are talking about.

Jesus was face-to-face with a similar language problem. The word causing the problem was *Messiah*. The Jewish people at the time of Jesus were expecting a Messiah, as they had for many years. But the kind of Messiah they expected was a very specific brand. They wanted a Messiah who would lead them in a political revolt against the Romans, who had conquered their country and were occupying it. The Jews felt that the Messiah would bring an easy life full of wealth and control over the rest of the world. This Messiah would have armies and would be unbeatable since

*More than Bread* / 49

God would be with him. He would do spectacular things, and eventually all the nations would bow to him and recognize him as the Messiah, the special messenger of God.

The kind of Messiah Jesus preached was a much different type of person. Jesus' Messiah would be humble and would have to suffer and die. The people couldn't understand that message.

What Jesus wanted to do, as Mark develops it, was to gradually lead the people to understanding and accepting *his* kind of Messiah, a Messiah that is entirely accurate in terms of the Old Testament tradition. He knew however, that if he immediately announced that he was the long-awaited Messiah, the crowd would think of *their* kind of Messiah, not his kind. So, he attempted to get his meaning across slowly. That's why he told people to keep quiet about his cures; he knew they would misinterpret their real significance.

The word *Messiah* means "the anointed one." It is a Hebrew word, and for all practical purposes it also means "king." The relationship between the Messiah and the reign or kingdom of God is very close: the kind of reign is determined by the kind of Messiah. It is interesting to note also that "Messiah" when translated into Greek becomes "Christ." Therefore, Jesus' complete name is not exactly Jesus Christ, as many people assume, but more accurately "Jesus *the* Christ." More than just his name, *Christ* is his "title-name."

The Messiah was not necessarily the Son of God; he did not have to be divine. In fact, God-becoming-man was foreign to the Jewish way of thinking. For them, there was just one God; his name was Yahweh, and he had no equals. It took the Jews many centuries to come to that belief, but by the time of Jesus it was firmly entrenched in their religious lives. They couldn't conceive of more than one God, let alone of a man as Son of God. That was blasphemy to them. So when they thought of the coming Messiah, they did not dream that the Messiah could also be God. Someone special, yes; but God, no!

It's a very difficult situation then for Jesus. He had to change their notion of Messiah, and he had to introduce them to the idea that the greatest thing God could do for man was to become man. Before his Resurrection, Jesus never did get his complete message across. He failed—until the Resurrection. And perhaps that was the only way in which he could truly succeed, by suffering and dying, a victim of the people's prejudices and of their inability to listen to his message, and a victim of everyone's involvement with evil.

## DISCUSSION TOPICS

*1) Almost everyone has seen street corner preachers or door-to-door evangelists, representing some religious group or other. Do you approve of this kind of missionary activity? Why or why not? Could you take part in such activity yourself? Jesus indicates in 6:7-11 that all Christians should be missionaries in some sense. How can you live out your type of missionary work?*

*2) Think of three or four members of your extended family— your parents, children, grandparents, brothers, sisters, aunts, uncles, cousins. Try to describe the kind of Jesus you think each one believes in. For example, one may think of Jesus as very stern; another may picture him as pleasant and cheerful; someone else may focus on the image of the Baby Jesus, etc. Describe these various images with as much detail as you can. Then compare these views of Jesus with the picture Mark gives of him in his gospel.*

*3) In the multiplication of the loaves (6:34-44), Jesus provides bread for a hungry crowd. Christians believe that the Eucharist satisfies one of our hungers, but that we need to be concerned about all kinds of hunger. For example, picture Bangledesh, India, Sahara, the aftermath of earthquakes, tornadoes, floods—places and events which remind us that there are millions of people who are physically hungry. What can you do to help?*

*4) The Hudsons are faithful Catholics: they participate in parish activities and programs; they never miss Mass on the weekend; they are relatively well-informed about current religious issues. But they have lost much of their enthusiasm about the Eucharist. Attending Mass and receiving Communion has become routine. What can they do to improve their participation in the Eucharist? How could you improve your own participation?*

PROJECTION INTO SPACE
by Mirtala Bentov
Courtesy, Pucker/Safrai Gallery, Boston

" . . . Jesus took with him Peter and James and John, and led them up a high mountain apart by themselves, and he was transfigured before them" Mark 9:2.

# FOUR
Mark 8:1-10:52

# What Kind of Messiah?

### INTERPRETING THE TEXT

The Secret is out. Someone finally recognizes Jesus as the Messiah or the Christ (Messiah is a Hebrew word; Christ is a Greek word with the same meaning). The someone is Peter. The place is Caesarea Philippi. It's not really a public pronouncement, as the only ones to hear it are the other eleven disciples. But it is the first real profession of faith in Jesus as the Messiah. More than likely, the episode at Caesarea Philippi was not just a sudden burst of insight on the part of Peter; he and the other disciples probably discussed the possibility of Jesus as Messiah before he makes this straightforward response when Jesus puts the question to him. It's not an admission of the divinity of Jesus, and the disciples still don't understand the kind of Messiah Jesus is; but it's a beginning. According to Mark, it's this kind of beginning Jesus was looking for.

Before this central event takes place, Mark recounts a few preparatory incidents. In one sense the first eight chapters of the gospel are preparing for Peter's statement; each previous episode is building towards this conclusion. But immediately preceding the confession at Caesarea Philippi, Mark records three significant incidents which in a particular and dramatic way lead into Peter's faith-statement. There is first of all the second account of the multiplication of the loaves. Secondly, there's a section describing the blindness of the disciples, and this is followed immediately with the story about the blind man of Bethsaida. It's with this climactic order that Mark dramatizes the importance of Peter's recognition of Jesus as the Messiah.

In Mark there are two accounts of the multiplication of the loaves. This repetition can be explained by the fact that the Christian community possessed two accounts of the event, and Mark, instead of choosing one of them, included both. The second account suited Mark because it is situated in Gentile territory, and he is particularly concerned about including the Gentiles within his gospel. As the Gentile version fits his theological purposes, he doesn't hesitate to write his gospel with two accounts of the multiplication of the loaves.

The Pharisees are not impressed with the signs Jesus has been giving them about his Messiahship. They ask for still another sign, but Jesus refuses since their motivation is to "test him," that is, to trap him. The sign they want corresponds to the kind of Messiah they expect, and in this way they are in opposition to him. Jesus works no such sign, implying that they don't have true faith in him, that their style of religion is a dead end, and that God will not work according to their demands.

The next section contains a stern rebuke to the disciples because they do not understand the meaning of the miracle of the loaves. The blindness of the disciples is evident in this passage. They forget to bring bread for the trip, an obvious allusion to the previous two episodes of the multiplication of the bread. They continue to think of the bread in a strictly physical sense, thereby missing the meaning of the message that Jesus is the bread of life. Jesus asks them to remember those two miracles with the hope that by remembering, they will see who he is, that is, recognize him as the Messiah.

The story of the curing of the blind man is similar to the story of the healing of the deaf-mute which followed the first account of the multiplication miracle. The cure here, as recorded by Mark, takes place gradually, the only place in the gospel where this happens. In the Old Testament it was stated that a sign of the Messiah would be that he would bring hearing to the deaf and sight to the blind. Following the first multiplication of the bread, Mark tells the story of Jesus bringing hearing to the deaf. Following the second account of the multiplication, Mark includes the cure of the blind man; Jesus brings sight to the blind. In effect then, these two healings are a sign of his Messiahship, fulfilling the prediction of the Old Testament.

The next passage (chapter 8, verses 27-30) is the turning point in the gospel of Mark. It's the hinge on which everything revolves. "Who do you say that I am?" It's the big question—the only question, really. The disciples proudly assert their fumbling faith: "You are the Messiah." Once the disciples, with Peter as their spokesman, recognize Jesus as the Messiah, the gospel proceeds with a renewed fervor, with a thrust and a vision that reverses man's usual sense of values. That new direction is introduced almost immediately: the Messiah will have to suffer. The disciples apparently did not understand this element of suffering, even as they admitted the Messiahship of Jesus. Jesus therefore still requires them to keep silent about who he is; he has to teach them further, correcting any false impressions they may have about his Messiahship. In a real sense, though, Jesus has been successful in his previous teaching. Other people don't even think of him as Messiah. To them he is John the Baptist or Elijah or someone else, but not the Messiah. Jesus' earlier decision to concentrate on teaching the disciples about his true identity is beginning to pay off in their recognition of him.

Immediately after Peter confesses to the Messiahship of Jesus, Mark includes the first prediction of the passion, death, and resurrection of Jesus. The purpose of this passage is obvious: Jesus must correct any false idea the disciples may have about the Messiah. He must attempt to give them some inkling of a suffering Messiah. These predictions have undoubtedly been reworked by the early Church and given their final form by Mark himself. It was only after the actual events of the passion and resurrection that the followers of Jesus could look back and say in effect, "Oh, yes, he did give us a hint that he was going to die and rise, but we really didn't believe it." As a result, the structure of these predictions has been formed by the faith and with the hindsight of the early Church. The evidence indicates however that Jesus himself did say something regarding his coming fate.

From this point on in the gospel, Jesus will refer to himself as "the Son of Man." This title comes from the Old Testament, and it refers primarily to the Jewish belief in the coming glory of a man who will act as judge of all nations. It indicates a glorious age for Israel. But the way Jesus uses this title adds another dimension to it. Jesus fuses the "Son of Man" with the notion of a "suffering Servant," another Old Testament title which many Jews conveniently forgot. In other words, Jesus accepts his identity, including the suffering it will entail.

Mark then makes it very plain that the disciples needed instruction on the meaning of Messiah. The same Peter who just a few verses earlier proudly professed his belief in the Messiahship of Jesus is here strongly rebuked because he tried to talk Jesus out of the necessity of suffering. Peter in effect plays Satan's role, tempting Jesus to compromise his mission, to submit to the power of evil. Jesus replies that he'll have none of it, that the only effective way to overcome the evil of suffering and death is to accept it and then to defeat it on its own terms.

This episode leads naturally into a series of sayings and incidents related to commitment and discipleship. The task of discipleship is not a half-hearted job; it is a demanding life of dedication. But those who accept it whole-heartedly will receive their reward, a purposeful meaning in this life and a completeness in the next life.

The transfiguration of Jesus is another one of those episodes which is hard to reconstruct as it actually happened. Apparently something happened which gave the favored disciples—Peter, James, and John—an insight into the glory of this Messiah-Jesus. It is connected with the profession of Peter at Caesarea Philippi; it is described as taking place "six days later," and therefore it is a way of clarifying the kind of Messiah Jesus was. Jesus has accepted the title of Messiah; he then insists that he must also suffer. But here in the transfiguration it is seen that the Messiah is equally a man of glory. This is a central event in describing the nature of Jesus' Messiahship.

The next episode is apparently a combination of a number of stories, put together by Mark in order to show Jesus' victory over the forces of evil. This miracle concludes the section begun by the first prediction of the Passion. The disciples play a special role, especially at the end, but the miracle is addressed to the crowds, who, even more than the disciples, are still missing the point of Jesus' message. As told here, the story is a prefigurement of Jesus' death and Resurrection (the boy became like a corpse), and an appeal for faith in Jesus. The disciples couldn't cast out the demon, probably because their usual method of doing so was by dialogue. The boy was a deaf-mute; therefore no dialogue was possible. They didn't know what to do. Jesus replies that they should pray. Perhaps their prayer was weak because their faith in Jesus was weak.

The second prediction of the Passion and Resurrection is

similar to the first. Mark repeats it in order to emphasize the significance of this teaching.

He then follows this second teaching with a long series of instructions on various topics. Each saying is an incident describing some aspect of discipleship and commitment to the reign of God. In a sense, this section might be characterized as a question and answer period, compiled by Mark from the source material he has available. Its purpose is to instruct the disciples, who still fail to understand the necessity of Jesus' suffering.

His instruction first emphasizes that the disciples are to serve others and not to be ambitious about their own prestige. Jesus manifests a very tolerant attitude towards those who expel demons but who do not officially belong to the disciples of Jesus. Previously the scribes and Pharisees attacked Jesus by saying that he drives out demons by the power of the devil. Here the disciples are making the same accusation of someone else. The response of Jesus is consistent with his earlier reply to the Jewish leaders: leave him alone; he's more with us than against us. Then Mark adds the important comment that helping people in seemingly little things like giving them a cup of water is a genuine act worthy of reward in the reign of God.

There follows immediately a series of sayings related to characteristics of a true follower of Jesus. Destroying the faith of others is directly opposed to the reign of God. Becoming ensnared in yourself, whether it's your hand, your foot, your eye, or any other part of you, leads you away from Jesus. Living according to the reign of God comes first, and that style of life demands concern for others; to concentrate selfishly on your own desires, to the detriment of other people, is not the behavior of a dedicated disciple. Mark concludes this series with the appeal to perseverance, that is, remain "salted" even under trying conditions (like persecution). Don't give up. The final word is a promise of peace to the disciples if they live out the attitudes just described. This instruction began with the disciples arguing with each other about who was the best among them. After the instruction they should be at peace with one another.

The question and answer period continues. This time the question centers on divorce. Jesus' view on the indissolubility of marriage is a new teaching. He insists on it without compromise, and by doing so he establishes his own authority even above the authority of Moses. Once a man and woman have been truly joined, they cannot be truly separated.

The next episode about the little children may be a reference to the Jewish custom of bringing the children to a scribe before the feast of the Day of Atonement for a blessing. The disciples object, probably because they don't want the parents to think of Jesus as a mere scribe. But Jesus uses the occasion for teaching a lesson: it is childlike confidence that makes it possible for a follower of Jesus to call God by his true title, that is, Father.

Jesus makes some strong statements about riches as well. The rich man comes to him asking a question, "How do I attain eternal life?" Jesus rebukes him a little, probably because the man wants an answer that would automatically assure him of eternal life. In effect, Jesus maintains that it's not easy. The man's priorities are still not consistent with the reign of God: he follows the commandments but his riches still come first. Jesus says that God must come first. The man is saddened because he didn't expect that kind of challenge, and he isn't ready to follow it. The strength of Jesus' teaching amazes and puzzles the disciples, particularly since the common Jewish thought was that riches were a sign of God's favor. The richer you were, the more God favored you. Jesus absolutely denies that principle. The bewilderment of the disciples is great, since Jesus' pronouncement is very severe. They therefore ask him about it, and he softens the teaching about riches by admitting that "with God" it is possible for a rich man to enter the reign of God. Peter then reminds Jesus that the disciples should be able to make it, since they are following him. Peter seems worried about living up to this difficult command of Jesus. Jesus, in turn, reassures the disciples that there are rewards for following him. But it's interesting that in the midst of the list of rewards Mark adds a note about persecution as well. He keeps the theme of suffering in mind even when he promises happiness. This mention of suffering leads into the third prediction of the Passion and Resurrection.

The third prediction is basically the same as the previous two, but there is an added tone. There's a feeling of immediacy present here: Jesus is on his way to Jerusalem, where it's all going to happen. He's walking ahead of the disciples, seemingly impatient to fulfill his mission.

The disciples continue to miss the message. This time the focus is on James and John, who ask for a personal place of honor, for prestige in the coming reign of God. They seem to accept the fact that suffering will be part of their discipleship, and as such that's an improvement in their understanding. But they're concentrating on their reward and doing so in a spirit of competition with the other disciples. In effect, Jesus repeats a previous teaching: in the reign of God disciples must serve one another, not dispute about who's the best among them. Those in authority must be servants to others. It's a service that Jesus, as the Suffering Son of Man, will push to its completeness by dying as an innocent victim for the sake of others.

The story about the disciples arguing over the places of honor is followed by the story of a blind beggar. The contrast is intended: the blind beggar seems to have the message of Jesus more clearly than the disciples. Jesus asks him the same question he asked James and John: "What do you want?" The beggar replies that he wants to see — a request for service. The disciples answered that they wanted prestige—an attitude unacceptable in the reign of God. This story of Bartimaeus is also a prelude to the next episode in the gospel, Jesus' triumphant entry into Jerusalem. The repeated acclamation about the Son of David is a title of great honor, and Jesus accepts it. There is no longer the command to keep silence since the end is so near anyway. Jesus commends the blind man for his faith, and like a true disciple the man begins to follow the Lord.

It's on that note of sight received and commitment to follow Jesus that this section of the gospel comes to an end. It is a fitting ending, since throughout these chapters Jesus has been trying to make the disciples see the necessity for his suffering and has been challenging them to commit themselves to follow in his path.

## SOME BACKGROUND NOTES

In general, people have always been believers. Primitive man believed in a spirit-world, a world existing beyond and behind a visible creation. The popularity and extension of the many world religions, both present and past, attest to the religious convictions of most human beings. People who have not aligned themselves to an organized religion oftentimes give evidence that they too are faith-people; they believe in something beyond themselves. The experience of faith has been with us since the beginning, is still present, and promises to remain a part of our life.

The gospel of Mark was written by a man of faith and intended to inspire faith in its readers. Faith is a dimension that cannot really be eliminated from the book. The gospel could be studied strictly as literature, but that approach would be like studying an automobile mechanic's manual as poetry. It doesn't really work; the purpose of the gospel is to witness to faith with the hope of eliciting faith in those who hear it.

The faith of the gospel is a specific kind of faith. It maintains, first of all, that there is a God. An atheist might read the gospel and be inspired by the concern Jesus showed to other people, by the courage and convictions he lived and died for, and by the loyalty of his followers. But an atheist would necessarily miss a crucial dimension of the gospel, namely, that there is a God who is concerned about man. The faith of the gospel goes further; it boldly states that Jesus of Nazareth is the Son of God, who offers to all men the hope that life has meaning, a meaning focused on Jesus. Mark's little book also insists that the Holy Spirit, sent by Jesus to be permanently present in this world, will continue to enliven mankind with the consistent message and power that God is with us, loving, forgiving, and saving us. It's this kind of belief that Mark gives testimony to, and it's out of this faith-framework that he writes his book.

The experience of faith has many qualities to it. It is primarily an experience; it is not just intellectually stating the propositions about God and Church which have been handed down to us. A person could state those ideas and not really experience them. A faith experience implies an acceptance by the whole person; mind, emotions, feelings, desires must all in some way participate in a genuine faith-experience. Such a faith-experience can be a very dramatic one-time episode, as St. Paul apparently experienced on the road to Damascus, when, shocked and blinded, he changed the direction of his life. Or a faith-experience can be a slowly developing sense of conviction, something that may take years and many contributing events. But genuine gospel faith is something that is lasting; it's not just a "spiritual high." It implies a way of life, a code of conduct, and a desire to renew and deepen the faith convictions. In terms of the gospel, faith means a consistently growing understanding that the Resurrection of Jesus provides meaning for a person's life. Jesus rose from the dead—that belief infiltrates the life of a gospel believer.

Jesus asks for faith from his followers. This is evident from almost every passage in the gospel. He works cures, but only on the condition that the recipient expresses some kind of faith in him. He spends hours, days, months with his disciples, giving them many opportunities to believe in him. He finally asks them point blank, "Who am I?" Peter responds with the faith statement that Jesus is the Messiah. Eliciting faith is one of Jesus' major concerns.

And yet Jesus never forces faith. He invites it, he encourages it, he points to the benefits a believer can lay claim to, but he doesn't take away the freedom of the potential believer. With every cure he asks for faith, but when his townspeople give no evidence of any faith in him, he "could work no miracles there." He is extremely patient with his disciples, even though they consistently miss his message. He does not force them. At one point, he confronts them very seriously with the ultimate statement of freedom: "Do you want to leave me also?" In other words, "You are free to go. Don't stay with me just because you feel you have to." Judas is one of his chosen twelve, and Jesus does not interfere with that follower's decision to betray the Master. Jesus respects the freedom of all men, and that respect is one of the amazing features of his relations with others.

For any faith to be genuine a similar atmosphere of freedom must be present. An individual must know the alternatives and freely choose to believe. The other disciples experienced this kind of freedom; they could either follow Jesus or reject him. It was up to them. Jesus simply offered himself, his message to them. Eventually he made that message clear to them, but he never forced them. Many other people heard Jesus, saw him, marveled at his message, and stood in amazement at his power, but quite obviously never became his disciples. They freely chose either to forget Jesus or to reject him. Whatever the case, Jesus did not chase after them and insist, for their own good, that they believe in him. He let them go. For Jesus, a faith commitment must be made freely, or else it runs the risk of not being genuine.

Another dimension of faith as described in the gospel of Mark is its communitarian feature. The individual must make his own personal faith decision, but oftentimes the individual is living in and influenced by a community. The disciples themselves were something of a community. They experienced Jesus together: they all walked with him and witnessed much of his life as a group. Undoubtedly they talked about Jesus among themselves—they compared insights and ideas, they were puzzled together, they were afraid together, and they misunderstood together. Jesus rebuked them as a group, and he taught them as a group. They were a community to the point of accepting Peter as their spokesman—or at least they did not object to having Peter speak for them. When Peter expressed his belief that Jesus was the Messiah, he did so in the name of the other eleven. He made his personal decision regarding Jesus, as presumably the other men did, but he made that faith commitment in the context of the community of the disciples.

An authentic gospel faith reflects this community dimension. No one is completely isolated from other people; we are social beings. Others influence us, some more than others. Family, friends, and even people we meet casually are all possible influences on our lives. In one form or another, Christians have always maintained this communitarian aspect of life. They experience Jesus that way, and they recognize that they need each other for mutual support and encouragement as they attempt to live their Christian lives ever more faithfully. That's why the early Christians formed communities wherever they were. They needed each other, and they believed that the Holy Spirit was present to them not just as individuals but as members of the community.

*What Kind of Messiah?* / 65

The gospel then, to be fully appreciated, must be read by a believer. The question Jesus confronted the disciples with—"Who do you say that I am?"—is a question directed to the reader as well as to the disciples. It's an inquiry that challenges, that puts us on the spot. But it's a question that respects our freedom while at the same time admitting our need for a community, for the influence and support of other people. It's a puzzling, demanding, crucial faith question.

Mark was a man of faith, and that faith influenced the writing of his gospel. But he was also a man of his times, in touch with current political and social events. It was a world controlled by the Romans politically and militarily, controlled rather well: there had not been a major war for a century. Besides, the Romans were wise and "good" conquerors. They certainly turned many people into slaves, but at the same time they left many nations a remarkable degree of independence. Local governments formed and operated by the people of the conquered country had the authority to govern their people on most local political and religious matters. The Romans were there as the final authority; they diligently kept their eyes on things. But they seriously tried not to interfere with most of the internal affairs of these smaller and weaker nations. The Romans reserved to themselves two particular facets of political life: first, they exercised the right to collect taxes; and, secondly, they made the final judgment regarding the death penalty.

Jesus and Mark lived under those social conditions. It was not the best of situations, but it was not the worst either. The Jewish people and their leaders had to respond to those conditions. Some Jewish leaders decided to go along with the Romans, to keep them happy, and to make the best of the situation. Others wanted to overthrow the Romans, to assume complete control of their country once again. This second group of Jews eventually engendered a deliberate, outright revolt against the Romans. Of course, the Romans grew impatient with these rebels and finally decided to put an end to their troublesome activities. In 70 A.D. Roman armies entered Judaea and within a relatively short period destroyed the nation after having leveled Jerusalem and the Temple.

The political events of Palestine obviously affected the early Christian Church. They were part of the social background out of which Mark wrote his gospel a few years before Jerusalem was destroyed. For some time after the Resurrection, the followers of Jesus considered themselves—and were viewed by others, the Romans included—as a sect or branch of Judaism. The disciples of Jesus continued to attend the Jewish synagogue, to worship in the Temple, and to observe many of the customary Jewish practices. In other words, they were Jews who followed the teaching of the Rabbi Jesus and who believed that this Rabbi was risen from the dead. Indications are that many of the early Jewish Christians wanted to maintain this very close connection with Judaism. Christian practice did not suddenly emerge as something brand new; it evolved rather slowly out of the Jewish faith.

In a relatively short time after the Resurrection of Jesus, Christian communities developed in cities of the Roman Empire outside of Palestine, especially at such places as Antioch, Damascus, Ephesus, Corinth, and Rome. These Gentile Christian communities were different from the Christian community in Jerusalem, the center of Judaeo-Christianity. The Gentile Christians did not see the need to be so closely identified with Jewish practices as did the Christians in Jerusalem. It was inevitable that factions began to form and that at some time or other they would clash. Eventually at a meeting in Jerusalem it was agreed that to be Christians new converts did not have to become Jewish first. The distinction between Judaism and Christianity thus became clarified.

Besides this internal, basic reason for the separation of Christianity from Judaism, there was an external, political one, the destruction of the Jewish nation mentioned above. Palestinian Christians did not want to be associated with the Jewish defeat and persecution. Many Christians were willing to accept suffering and persecution but not because they were considered Jews who were fighting the Romans. Being persecuted for Christ was different from being persecuted as a Jewish political revolutionary. As a result, Christians insisted that they were not really Jews; they were something different. At the time this approach seemed to work; for the most part the Christians were spared during this persecution. The Romans admitted a distinction between Christianity and Judaism.

## DISCUSSION TOPICS

*1) When Jesus multiplies the loaves of bread (8:1-9), he feeds everyone who is present. At our Eucharistic celebrations today there are rules which determine who may and who may not receive Communion. Suppose you became involved with a group of people who represent a number of local Christian churches. The purpose of the group is to help improve the living conditions for the elderly in your area. You're delighted that members of various Christian denominations work together so well on this project. You think the group should also worship together. In this kind of situation, should Christians of different churches be officially allowed to receive Communion together? Discuss this issue.*

*2) Peter's act of faith in Jesus as Messiah (8:27-30) is far from final. At this point his concept of Messiah is incomplete. We are often faced with what can be called partial acts of faith. Discuss* this situation: *Bob Calhoun is a successful businessman in his mid-50's. He is a graduate of a Catholic university, active in his parish, and self-assured in the fact that he was able to study theology while in college. As a young man he became convinced that he had "the faith" and that he had learned it for life.* How would you try to convince Bob that faith-acts need to be updated and repeated throughout life? How would you encourage him to learn more about the faith? Is a person less a believer when he questions his faith? Are there any aspects of belief that should not be questioned?

3) Throughout the gospel Jesus spends a great deal of time teaching people about the reign of God. One example of this teaching can be found in Mark 9:30-10:45. Today, however, a basic problem often arises. You have probably heard someone say: "The Bible is important, but there are so many interpretations that I don't know who or what to believe!" How can we solve this problem? Who represents the true teaching of Jesus today? How do you know true teaching from false teaching?

4) In every period of history the relationship between wealth and poverty has led to wars, exploitation, jealousy, murder, discrimination, and other forms of injustice. This raises many moral questions. For example, what is the Christian attitude toward wealth (10:17-31)? Is wealth a sign of God's favor? Do poor people have an advantage in God's kingdom? Should a wealthy person give his/her money to the poor? Do the poor have a right to demand a share in the wealth?

**METROPOLIS**
by Mirtala Bentov
Courtesy, Pucker/Safrai Gallery, Boston

"And they came to Jerusalem. And he entered the temple and began to drive out those who sold and those who bought in the temple" Mark 11:15.

# FIVE
# Mark 11:1-13:37

# Avoiding the Trap

## INTERPRETING THE TEXT

Jesus arrives in Jerusalem—the first time he's been in that city, according to Mark. His arrival and his activities there are adapted to Mark's purpose and the development of his gospel. Jerusalem is the place of conflict and crucifixion. To read just Mark's gospel, one would get the impression that Jerusalem was a very evil city. The other evangelists treat the city much more favorably, probably because, once again, they are writing to a Jewish Christian audience, an audience that had strong emotional ties to Jerusalem. Not so for Mark or his Gentile readers. For him, Jerusalem is the setting for Jesus' seeming failure.

Jesus enters the city triumphantly. But the acclamation of the crowd is not necessarily a profession that Jesus is the Messiah. Rather, the crowd is hailing the future reign of David's son. In other words, the cheering crowd recognizes Jesus as a forerunner to some other king who is to come at a time which they feel is near. And yet Jesus is claiming some Messiahship by this action. The contrast between Jesus' Messiah and the crowd's Messiah is still in evidence. But Jesus seeks to teach by his entry into Jerusalem. He is not a man of war. He is humble and lowly, riding on an ass. Those celebrating his arrival are probably a little puzzled, but perhaps they begin to get the message: Jesus is not the Messiah of their hopes, but he is still a Messiah.

Mark dramatizes this entry into Jerusalem by stressing the religious nature of the event rather than its political overtones. No doubt both themes were present in the original happening, but with the description of the detailed preparations for the arrival and the spreading of the garments and branches on the ground, the deliberate intent of Mark is to emphasize the religious significance of the event. The cry of "hosanna" also adds to the liturgical dimension of the entry, putting the political implications into the background.

It's impossible to determine when Jesus cleansed the Temple of the moneylenders. But in Mark's plan this is the right place for it. It's quite clear what Jesus is doing here: exercising his authority as Messiah to condemn the abuses of the Temple and to challenge the people to return to the purity of intention and devotion for which the Temple was originally built. The chief priests and scribes naturally objected and wanted to get rid of this meddlesome carpenter from the hill country of Galilee.

Following the events of Jesus' entry into Jerusalem, the cursing of the fig tree, and the cleansing of the Temple, Mark continues to depict Jesus in conflict with the scribes and Pharisees. The struggle is mounting in intensity; the condemnations are stronger. Jesus becomes more and more fearless, and the Jewish leaders become more and more drastic in their designs to destroy him. Jesus walks right into the Temple area, knowing that a confrontation was inevitable. The Jewish leaders quickly gathered and angrily put the big question to him: "Who do you think you are, doing all these things?" It's the right question, really, but the intention of the leaders is to trap Jesus. So he cleverly turns the tables on them, exposing their real purpose. They're afraid of the crowds, who still admire John the Baptist. But if they admit that John was a true prophet, then they would be guilty because they refused to listen to John. Therefore they back down. Jesus replies that if they don't know who he is by now, and by what authority he preaches, they will never know.

Jesus then preaches, using a parable to get his point across. Based on an Old Testament text from the book of Isaiah, the parable recounts the story of the plight of an owner of a vineyard. The vineyard stands for Israel, the owner is God, the tenants are the religious leaders of Israel, the servants are the prophets, and the son, of course, is Jesus. In other words the fate the prophets met (most of them were killed or at least rejected by the leaders) is the same fate awaiting Jesus. The question is logical and inevitable: "What will that owner do?" He will judge and condemn those tenants; the vineyard will no longer be theirs to work. The message is clear: God will reject the Old Israel and establish a New Israel, a people who recognize Jesus as the true Messiah.

The Jewish leaders leave and plot their next move. They have been embarrassed and challenged, and they realize they have to be very clever to trap Jesus. They decide to send two opposing groups to him, the Pharisees, who are to some degree tolerant of the Romans, and the Herodians, who object to the Roman occupation. They try to flatter Jesus in an attempt to catch him off guard. They pose a problem to him, one which appears to be impossible to answer correctly. If he gives one answer, the Pharisees will object; if he gives the other response, the Herodians will attack him. Armed with this strategy, they approach Jesus. He sees through their flattery and dismisses it immediately. He pulls the rug out from under their whole plot by giving a response they haven't even thought about. They're left speechless and defeated once again.

But they immediately regroup and try yet another approach.

The Sadducees now come forward and offer their services. They have a question which they believe Jesus could never answer. The problem of the resurrection of the body was a difficult one, and one on which the Jews themselves were divided. The Sadducees rejected belief in the resurrection, and the situation they presented to Jesus was designed to ridicule that belief and to show that the written law of Moses did not allow for the resurrection of the body. It was a trap question again. If Jesus sided with the Sadducees, then the Pharisees could discredit him. If he sided with the Pharisees, then the Sadducees could lead the public condemnation of him. In other words, the Jewish leaders are trying desperately to get some seemingly legal ground to launch their attack against Jesus. They cannot kill him outright because the Romans have the final word on the death penalty. They cannot assassinate him because the crowds are then likely to rebel and make Jesus a martyr. They must discredit Jesus to the crowds and at the same time establish a legal foundation for their appeal to Pilate for the death penalty. That's why they continually try to trap him. In this instance Jesus simply states that after death our relationships will be different from those we have here on earth. Therefore their question about the resurrection of the body shows a lack of understanding. Scripture says that God—who is the God of the living—is the God of Abraham, of Isaac, and of Jacob. Therefore, these three patriarchs must still be living. The implication is that the Old Testament indicates a belief in the Resurrection. The Sadducees are thus also defeated in their verbal conflict with Jesus.

The next confrontation is much more friendly in tone. It seems that at least one of the scribes is genuinely impressed with Jesus and asks a serious question, not to trap him but simply to get an answer. One of the tasks of a scribe was to determine the most significant commands of the Old Testament and rank them in the order of importance. Naturally, this caused differences of opinion among the scribes. Jesus' contribution to this discussion was not unique in that he singled out the two commands to love God and love neighbor. But what is unique about Jesus' approach is that he combines these two commands, putting them side by side, as two parts of a single moral principle. Jesus praises the scribe, who accepts Jesus' interpretation. The other Jewish leaders obviously don't like this teaching, but they're afraid to confront Jesus any more because he consistently outmaneuvers them, exposing their lack of real faith.

The controversy now switches. Instead of merely answering the problems posed by the religious leaders, Jesus now takes the initiative and raises a number of questions for them. Jesus is on the attack. He goes right to the heart of the problem, namely, the kind of Messiah they are expecting. It was commonly held that the Messiah would come from the tribe of David and be a king like David. Jesus maintains that being a blood descendant of David is not the important point. No, the Messiah would be much greater even than King David. And since he's greater than David, his reign can be different but greater than David's reign. The crowd enjoys this because the Pharisees can't answer.

The climax of this section comes as Jesus attacks the hypocrisy of his opponents. These men put on a good show and demand respect from those less fortunate than themselves. They view themselves as being in a superior position in the Jewish community. But Jesus condemns them for their pride, their hypocrisy, and their practice of confiscating the savings of widows in the form of a Temple tax.

The mention of the widow inspires Mark to add one final story. The lot of widows in Jewish society was an extremely difficult one. Mark uses this incident to praise the "lowly" and to demonstrate the true spirit of almsgiving. In the context of this section of the gospel, it's also a condemnation of the Pharisees who have just been criticized for their show-off approach to religious practices. The real worth of an offering should be judged according to the sacrifice involved, not the amount given. Another implication of these few verses is that Jesus will soon offer himself as a sacrifice, seemingly a poor offering but in reality a great sacrifice.

The stage is now set for the next dramatic act in Mark's gospel. After an interlude about the coming reign of God, the passion narrative unfolds. The opposing sides are clearly drawn. The forces of evil will soon make their final all-out attack on Jesus. As always, he confronts them courageously.

Chapter 13 of the gospel of Mark may be the most difficult section for the modern reader to appreciate. There's a style of writing here that's unfamiliar to many people in the twentieth century. Perhaps this style is something like a combination of poetry, science fiction, preaching, exhortation, and prediction. Technically it's called the apocalyptic style, and, needless to say, it was much more common at the time of Mark. Mark didn't use it very often, but he does employ it here. As a result, this passage is easily misinterpreted.

What may be helpful in reading this discourse of Jesus is to remember that there are two themes, two perspectives, usually presented at the same time. The one topic concerns the coming destruction of Jerusalem; the other theme deals with the second coming of Jesus, under the title of the Son of Man. These two predictions are interwoven: in one verse Mark may refer to the destruction of Jerusalem and in the very next verse switch to the Son of Man. And sometimes the author puts the two themes together. Our task will be to identify when he writes about Jerusalem and when he's referring to the second coming. In both instances Jesus is exhorting his disciples to be vigilant, to be on their guard, to be ready for both events.

The opening comment by one of the disciples regarding the size of the Temple sets the stage for this discourse. Later in the gospel, Jesus will be accused before the Jewish ruling body of planning to destroy the Temple, an accusation which is a gross misinterpretation of Jesus' comment here. At the time of Jesus, the Temple was still under construction, and it was completed just seven years before the Romans destroyed it. The prediction by Jesus was fulfilled in 70 A.D. This prediction then serves as a springboard for the rest of the discourse.

In verses 3-8, Jesus looks beyond the physical destruction of the Temple to the signs preceding the coming of the Son of Man. The coming fate of the Temple and the city of Jerusalem is not forgotten; it's still present in the background of these verses, but the focus concentrates on the broader vision about the future of mankind.

The discourse, in verses 9-13, centers on the Christian disciple and is an exhortation to remain firm in the faith. The Christians will be persecuted in the synagogues, that is, by the Jewish leaders, and will be brought before governors and kings, that is, they will also be persecuted by the Gentiles. In these crises, Jesus assures his followers that they will not be alone, that the Spirit will be with them. By the time Mark wrote this gospel, it was certainly true that Christians were hated because of the name of Jesus. This brief section ends with the repeated appeal for vigilance.

The next nine verses concentrate on the coming destruction of the Temple. Indications are that Mark wrote this before the actual happening in 70 A.D. Even though he was living in Rome when he composed this text, he was more than likely aware of the political situation in Israel. The reference in verse fourteen to the "desolating sacrilege" is most accurately interpreted as an indication of a foreign army occupying the Temple, particularly the inner sanctuary.

The focus now switches to the coming of the Son of Man in glory. These verses (24-27) look beyond the physical destruction of the Temple and describe the time of the final victory of God. The imagery here is almost entirely taken from the Old Testament. The time of this event is left open; there is no way to predict it accurately. The message here maintains that the Son of Man will act as judge, bringing calm after the calamities and order to the chaos. He will claim his kingdom and exercise his power as ruler.

The discourse ends with repeated exhortations to vigilance (verses 28-37). Mark in this closing passage refers to both the destruction of Jerusalem and the second coming of Jesus. Mark seems to think that both events will happen in the relatively near future, but he doesn't really know exactly when. No one knows except the Father. In any case, the Christian is to be ready, regardless of when the second coming takes place. This appeal for proper preparation is made to all men, in all generations, and as such it's obviously an appeal which goes far beyond the warning regarding the coming destruction of the city and Temple of Jerusalem.

## SOME BACKGROUND NOTES

Jewish society was a theocracy, a form of government that made little or no distinction between politics and religion. Every phase of life in Israel was theoretically ruled by God. Government officials were representatives of God; that's why, at the time of Jesus, the High Priest had such great power, both political and religious. A violation of civil law was a sin against Yahweh, and the Law of Moses reigned supreme in government. To betray the country was to betray God. To be a "fallen-away" Jew was not only heresy but treason as well. The Romans, then, as the final political power in the land, were resented because their presence challenged the very fiber of the Jewish politico-religious society.

It's no wonder that to a Jew the Romans were not just conquerors; they were heretics, destroyers, perpetual enemies.

Along with the Romans came the Greeks, if not actually in person, then certainly in their thought, culture, and philosophy. The Romans conquered the Greeks militarily, but in time the Greeks repaid the compliment by conquering the Romans culturally. Rome was strong on armies, law, roadbuilding, and governmental organization, but weak in philosophy, culture, art, theology, and a "graceful" style of life. The Greeks supplied these missing elements to such an extent that the ideal man in the Roman empire was more Greek than Roman. This Greek cultural influence, known as Hellenism, swept across the Empire, gaining new converts in every land to the Greek way of thinking. It was inevitable that Hellenism would clash head-on with Judaism.

At the time of Mark the Jews were divided: some favored the Greek style and believed it could be incorporated within Judaism. Others strenuously objected, insisting that any compromise with the Hellenists was a sinful betrayal of the Law of Moses. This difference of opinion, plus the unresolved debate regarding the presence of the Romans (some Jews wanted to appease the Romans; others wanted to kill them), and other social and religious factors created a Jewish society that was highly complex. The first century A.D. found many factions within that society, oftentimes at odds with each other and very near to civil war. That new religious sect, the Christians, only complicated matters more.

Reading the Gospels, we get glimpses of these factions and groups within Judaism. The Pharisees, the Sadducees, the scribes, and the chief priests all make many appearances in the gospels. Who are all these people, and what do they stand for? Let's take a look at some of them. It's important to remember, however, that we're not dealing with different political parties here—at least not in the sense that Americans know political parties. Nor are they really different "religious sects," such as Catholics and Lutherans. More to the point would be to say that these groups of people are like our liberals and conservatives. And yet, this type of classification is not completely satisfactory either. What we are referring to in these classifications are schools of thought or philosophies of life or differing value systems. They are very real in that they affect almost every aspect of an individual's life, from his thoughts to his feelings and from the type of job he accepts to the people he socializes with. These categories may help to unravel some of the complexities of the Jewish society reflected in the gospel of Mark.

We begin with the Sadducees. They were the aristocrats, the ruling class—the rich, arrogant, "jet-set" of Palestinian society. They were Hellenized, probably because they traveled more and were acquainted with foreign customs. Their view was international; they were familiar with the workings of the Roman Empire and the court life of the Emperor. Within Judaism the Sadducees were the official heads of organized religion. They carried out their rituals and ceremonies with great exactness and pride, but they accepted only the written Old Testament with a special emphasis on the first five books of Moses. This belief put them in opposition to the Pharisees, who believed in the oral interpretations of the Scriptures as well as the written texts. Sadducees interpreted the Law of Moses literally and exactly, with a strong concentration on the laws regarding ritual purification. Intellectually, they doubted many commonly-held Jewish beliefs: they denied the resurrection of the body, the existence of spirits other than Yahweh, and a life after death. Their God was not concerned about man. They had little contact with the people, and although they were the rulers, they were not the real leaders of the people. They were the High Priests, but they were rejected by the people because of their arrogance, their cooperation with the Romans, their wealth, and their acceptance of the Greek way of thinking.

Then there were the scribes. The scribes were teachers, and as such their influence on the masses of the people was great. They were held in great respect because they spent many years studying the Law, and the Jewish crowds felt that *all* knowledge was contained somewhere in Scripture. The scribes would study the Law for so long and with such intensity that they could recite from memory not only the written Bible but an enormous amount of interpretations of that Law as well. Ordinarily a man would not be accepted as a true scribe until he was about thirty years old, and it's quite possible that Jesus delayed his public ministry until he was the acceptable age. Scribes were not necessarily Pharisees, but many of them were. Scribes were teachers of the Law; Pharisees were strict observers and followers of that Law. It was the duty of the scribes to keep the Law alive for the people, and generally they accomplished this task. They spelled out the demands of the Law in great detail, but they also knew the loopholes and felt no scruples about using those loopholes. Their concentration on the Law led them to believe in the absolute necessity of observing the letter of the Law. External conformity to the Law, regardless of what the inner spirit or motivation of the person might be, was the avenue for achieving salvation. It is precisely on this point that Jesus challenged the scribes.

The Pharisees were followers of the Law as spelled out by the scribes. The Pharisees were a "hard-nosed" group: strictly Jewish and opposed to both Roman government and Greek style of thought and life. They endured the Romans, offering them passive resistance, simply because they didn't know what else to do about it. To them Hellenism was a terrible evil and should be eliminated from Judaism. The Pharisees were aloof and snobbish towards the people. This arrogance had its roots in the belief that the only true Jew was one who followed the precepts of the Law as exactly as the Pharisees did. And most of the people of the land could not or would not live according to those exacting regulations. The Pharisees then thought they were better than most men, and they apparently seldom hesitated to let people know how "good" they were. The Pharisees were extremely careful to fulfill all the rituals regarding temple worship. They also believed that all knowledge was contained in the Scriptures and in the accepted interpretations of the Old Testament. The Pharisees were respected for their so-called piety, and they worked hard to convert others. Some of them followed Jesus, but the impression we get is that most of the Pharisees were legalists, performing external actions without too much internal devotion or intention. They were not a political party, but they were a powerful group, since they, along with the scribes, were considered ideal Jews. They believed in the immortality of the soul, the resurrection of the body, the providence of God, and the free will of men. These beliefs put them in direct opposition to the Sadducees.

A number of other groups can be identified within Jewish society. The Essenes, though not directly mentioned in the Gospels (some scholars speculate that John the Baptist may have been closely connected with this group), were a monastic-like community living in the desert near the Dead Sea. Their beliefs and life-style are described in the famous Dead Sea scrolls. In a sense, they were a radical fringe of society, practicing an austere life of total devotion to the Law of Moses and believing in the exclusive favor of God to the Jews. A group known as the Zealots, on the other hand, were politically active, even to the point of pursuing open revolution against the Romans. Barabbas was probably a Zealot. The publicans worked for the Romans as tax-collectors and were generally despised by the people because many of them seemed to be corrupted by bribery and extortion. Then there were the "people of the land," the common people leading ordinary lives, without positions or political power. They were the farmers, the shepherds, the peasants. Some of them were further classified as the poor, including the widows, the orphans, and those heavily in debt. The blind, the beggars, the bandits were labeled the outcasts. Samaritans were usually rejected by Jews because Samaritans had mixed blood: they were the descendants of marriages between Jews and Gentiles.

A final word could be added about the Diaspora. These were faithful Jews, about two and one-half million of them, who lived outside of Palestine in all the major cities of the Mediterranean Basin. These Jews kept close contact with Jerusalem. Their relationships to their pagan neighbors often seemed to be strained, even though the Diaspora Jews attempted to adapt themselves to their surroundings as much as they could. It was this group that translated the Old Testament from Hebrew into Greek, the most common language of the Roman Empire. It was also this group of Jews living outside of Israel that St. Paul visited and preached to when he made his missionary journeys.

Jewish society, then, was complex. The preceding classifications are simplifications—not every Pharisee, not every Sadducee, nor every publican fits into these neat categories. But this overview of Jewish society at the time of Jesus and Mark can provide us with some helpful background as we read Mark's account of the life, death, and Resurrection of Jesus.

## DISCUSSION TOPICS

*1) Jesus was questioned about the source of his authority as teacher, prophet, and healer (11:27-28). The issue of authority is still with us. In a democracy we believe that final political authority comes from the people. In the Catholic Church we say that, in a special way, authority resides in the pope and the bishops. Can we reconcile these two views of authority? How? How are these two approaches to authority related to the statement: all authority comes from God?*

*2) Can you identify any modern day prophets? Mother Teresa of Calcutta? Don Helder Camara? Ralph Nader? Others? In a sense, we are all called to be prophets, to speak out courageously for what we know is right even when our stand is unpopular. To what extent are you a prophet?*

*3) Sheila Harrison has believed in the divinity of Jesus since childhood. As she got older, this belief has grown in importance, and today it is central to her faith. Her first thought of Jesus is that He is God. Recently, however, she was disturbed by a homily she heard on the humanity of Jesus. The preacher said that Jesus was fully human, that he had a human intellect and will, and human emotions just like the rest of us. To illustrate his point the speaker referred to the cleansing of the Temple (11:15-18) and to the fact that Jesus was a descendant of King David (12:35-37). Sheila feels that this kind of talk makes Jesus too much like us. How would you respond to her?*

*4) The Temple was sacred to the Jews, yet Jesus said that it would be destroyed (13:1-4). What are the things that are sacred to you? Would you let them be destroyed? "Everyone has a price," or so the saying goes. The price is not just money, as it could be prestige, acceptance, fame, popularity, etc. When it comes to your religion, are there some things you would refuse to let be destroyed regardless of the rewards?*

### FREEDOM FROM MATTER
by Mirtala Bentov
Courtesy, Pucker/Safrai Gallery, Boston

"And he said to them, 'Do not be amazed, you seek Jesus of Nazareth, who was crucified. He is risen, he is not here'" Mark 16:6.

# SIX
# Mark 14:1-16:20

# Death and Resurrection

## INTERPRETING THE TEXT

The story of the Passion and death of Jesus is familiar to most Christians. They have heard it before. Hearing it again and again has been profitable to many people; they testify to the fact that although the account doesn't change, they do. As a result the same story means different things to them; it strikes them differently during various readings of the text.

Mark's narrative of the Passion and death is probably closest to the actual happening. It's remarkable in its simplicity and in its disciplined desire to stick to the facts. There are scenes of great emotion, but those emotions are clearly and simply stated without elaborate detail. There is drama in the account, as there undoubtedly was in the event itself, but that drama is presented in a low-key fashion. This section is the climax of Mark's gospel, building to the centurion's comment, "Truly this man was the Son of God!" But Mark immediately moves on, content that in that one short sentence he has adequately summarized what he has been trying to say since the beginning. Jesus is finally recognized publicly as the Messiah, but as a suffering Messiah. This account is not history as we generally understand it, since

Mark includes a theological interpretation of the events he is describing. And yet he tells his story very simply.

The Passion narrative begins with a statement regarding the intention of the Jewish leaders to kill Jesus. They must be careful, however; Jesus is in town, but so are many other Jews, including many from Jesus' home territory of Galilee. The leaders are understandably worried about the reaction of these crowds.

The anointing at Bethany is somewhat of an interruption of the Passion narrative. But Mark justifies its presence here by interpreting the incident as an anointing for Jesus' burial. The comment about the poor is not a call to neglect the needs of those in poverty; it is rather a comment which emphasizes the brief lifespan of Jesus. The woman is praised for recognizing this fact and for expressing her love.

The Passion narrative continues with Judas joining forces with the enemies of Jesus. They are happy since Judas could supply them with the information they needed: the time and place when Jesus would be alone with no large crowds around to defend him. Judas is one of the Twelve, a close associate of Jesus. His betrayal is therefore that much more horrifying.

The Last Supper is presented in three phases: the preparations for the Passover meal, the announcement of the betrayal, and the Eucharist. Jesus' last meal is the Passover celebration, an annual event remembering the Jewish Exodus from Egypt. It provided a formal religious setting for the Jews to express their thanks to Yahweh and to rededicate themselves to the covenant originally made on Mount Sinai. The purpose of this meal in the life of Jesus is to show that Jesus identifies himself as our Passover, as one who goes through the process of death to achieve the freedom of new life. This meal is a perfect setting for Jesus to accomplish what he intends.

Mark, in recounting the Eucharist, formulated the event for

the purpose of inspiring Christian faith and worship. The formulation of the ceremony is liturgical. At the beginning of the main course Jesus blesses the bread and declares that this bread is his body, that is, himself. Likewise later in the meal he takes a cup of wine, most likely the third cup of the Passover meal, and proclaims this cup of wine as his blood. It's a reference to the covenant made by Moses on Mt. Sinai, and, since blood indicates the life of a person or an animal, the point here is that Jesus will "pour out" his life for others. That "pouring out" will be bloody when he dies on the cross; it is unbloody during this meal. Through these actions Jesus establishes a New Covenant, which is similar to the Sinai agreement but much more extensive, and which will be concluded at the Messianic banquet in the future final reign of God.

On the way to Gethsemane Jesus says that the disciples will leave him during the coming crisis. This act of desertion follows the continual misunderstanding the disciples have exhibited throughout the gospel; it's no wonder that it could lead to cowardice.

Arriving at the garden, Jesus wants some time alone. He suffers the deep pain of decision-making. The psychological suffering that he undergoes in the garden seems to leave him once he firmly and resolutely accepts the cross; after this episode he seems calm and courageous throughout all his physical suffering of the next day. The three disciples, Peter, James and John, are the same three who witnessed the transfiguration and the raising of Jairus' daughter. They had seen his glory and were amazed. They are now invited to be with him in his loneliness and suffering, but they don't support him. The distress Jesus feels is so real and so painful that he wants to die; death would be a relief. But throughout this deep depression Jesus still addresses God as Father. This indicates his continued trust in the midst of his agony and his confidence in the Father even as the horror of his crucifixion almost overwhelms him. At the end he calmly faces his destiny alone. The disciples' continued sleepiness highlights the tension and loneliness felt by Jesus.

Judas makes his appearance, still addressed ironically as one of the Twelve. His traitorous act is emphasized by his misuse of the embrace, an act which symbolizes friendship. It was dark in the garden, and the people sent to arrest Jesus apparently did not know who he was. Judas was needed to point out the right man. Jesus confronts them with logic, exposing their true motives. They didn't have the courage to arrest him when he was with them at the Temple. The disciples slip off into the darkness, and Jesus is left alone.

The Sanhedrin was seeking testimony against Jesus. This action was needed to establish some legal ground for asking Pilate for the death penalty. There were no prosecuting or defense attorneys in Jewish court procedures. Witnesses were simply brought forward, and if two of them agreed, the case against the defendant was made. The defendant then could speak in his own defense. In Jesus' case the witnesses couldn't agree, and according to Mark they lied. The accusation about the destruction of the Temple was a complete misunderstanding of Jesus' earlier comments. The high priest had to interrupt, taking a very unusual and possibly illegal action. Jesus' silence may have simply been the most obvious response to the lack of agreement among the witnesses. But the high priest is determined to convict Jesus; he asks him a question about his identity. That identity is precisely what Jesus has been trying to establish since the beginning of his ministry. He therefore responds. Only the king could be called the anointed one of Israel. Jesus explains his answer with allusions to the Old Testament, the net effect being that he identifies himself with the one who sits at the right hand of God and acts as judge in the reign of God. He shares in the glory of God.

The High Priest tears his garment, a sign of formal disapproval and judgment against the defendant. The charge is blasphemy, ordinarily punished by stoning. The agreement by the rest of the Sanhedrin implies that the whole nation of Israel is rejecting Jesus. They immediately begin to punish him.

The overall impression of this "trial" as recorded in Mark is that Jesus didn't have a chance.

Peter's denial probably took place during the night. The three-fold betrayal builds in intensity: at first he claims ignorance, then makes a simple denial, and finally denies Jesus with vehemence. The point is that when he betrays Jesus, he does it deliberately. But Mark is quick to report that he repents vehemently also.

The Sanhedrin now moves to Pilate, in order to get his permission to kill Jesus. Pilate asks Jesus if he is the king of the Jews. The emphasis in this interrogation is not on the religious dimension of the title of king; before Pilate Jesus is not accused of blasphemy. The stress here is on the political overtones connected with the title of king—politics was a concern of Pilate, particularly if the possibility of rebellion was involved. The answer that Jesus gives is a little vague, but it probably amounts to an admission that he is king, although he would phrase the question much differently.

The mention of Barabbas and the custom of releasing a prisoner at Passover time emphasizes the presence of a crowd hostile to Jesus and dramatizes the embarrassing situation Pilate is in. The effect of the incident is to show the great responsibility of the chief priests for Jesus' crucifixion. The involvement of Pilate is not emphasized; he's described as trying to save Jesus. In the end, however, he gives in to the crowd, and his responsibility is clearly stated.

To the soldiers Jesus is just another prisoner, and they enjoy the cruelty of mocking him while they prepare the execution. Jesus suffers as "king."

The crucifixion is described in almost matter of fact terms, in a tone that seems impersonal. Simon and his sons Alexander and Rufus are possibly Christians known to the Gentile Church. It's quite likely that Jesus needed help carrying the cross, since he had just been scourged. Golgotha was a place probably so named because it was a hill shaped like a skull. The exact spot is difficult to determine since the city of Jerusalem was destroyed in 70 A.D. and then again in 135 A.D. But it's not likely that all Christians of those times forgot the place of the crucifixion. Mark's account says simply, "They crucified him." The mention of the dividing of Jesus' clothing recalls Psalm 22 of the Old Testament. The penalty Jesus was finally accused of was claiming he was "King of the Jews." The inscription came from Pilate and emphasized the political overtones implied in the title.

Darkness comes at noon, fulfilling the Old Testament prophecy that the land will be dark when Yahweh appears. Jesus prays in the words of Psalm 22, a psalm which includes this passage of seeming despair but which in its totality is an expression of trust in God and of consolation in times of suffering. The crowd on the hill misunderstood his words, even to the point of referring to Elijah. At the very end of his life Jesus cries out, possibly in pain; death comes violently. Some commentators regard this cry as a shout of freedom in which Jesus delivers his life to the Father. The curtain in the sanctuary of the Temple was torn in two: this detail signified the end of the Old Israel and the beginning of the new, a time when the death of Jesus is the avenue to reach the Father. In contrast with the Jews, a Gentile—a Roman army officer at that—expresses his belief in the identity of Jesus. What this soldier meant by "Son of God" is debatable; what Mark meant by it when he wrote the gospel is clearer. This statement is the climax of the gospel and attests to the divinity of Jesus.

## Death and Resurrection / 93

The mention of the people present at the crucifixion is an anticipation of the next chapter, when some of these women will go to Jesus' tomb in order to anoint him for burial.

The account of the burial of Jesus confirms the fact that he died. Courageously Joseph of Arimathea makes the arrangements. Pilate's acceptance of the death of Jesus is similar to the official death announcement. Jesus is not just unconscious, in a coma, or too weak to respond. He is medically, physically, legally, officially, and completely dead. Under the circumstances, the burial is understandably hasty; there is no funeral ceremony and certainly no crowd. Even the Apostles are absent. The presence of the women explains how they knew where Jesus was buried.

On this note the Passion narrative according to Mark is concluded.

The tomb is empty. Three women discover this unexpected situation when they go to anoint the body of Jesus. They are told to spread the word to the disciples, who are to meet Jesus in Galilee. But the women become frightened and they don't tell anyone.

Thus ends the gospel according to Mark. It's an abrupt ending, so abrupt that many people believe that the complete ending of Mark's gospel has been lost. Verses 1-8 in this final chapter are the work of Mark himself, but verses 9-20 were added by someone else at a later time. The vocabulary and the style of writing in this last section indicate that the composer of these last eleven verses was not Mark. Who this author was we don't know, but the date of composition was sometime in the first or second century. This passage is accepted however as a truly inspired part of the gospel message.

The precision and detail of the Passion narrative evaporate when it comes to the various accounts of the Resurrection. No evangelist records the actual rising. They concentrate on two related themes: the discovery of the empty tomb and the appearances of Jesus after his death. Compared with the story of the death of Jesus, this approach to the Resurrection may seem surprising. The Resurrection and the Ascension are the crowning events of his life—the unique, astounding experience of life after death made visible to his disciples. One would expect precision and detail in recording this Resurrection event. But it's not there. Apparently the early Church felt no need for one coordinated Resurrection account, although they felt a need for a coordinated Passion account.

The women went to the tomb obviously to honor the dead. They delayed their arrival not because they couldn't anoint a corpse on the Sabbath but because they couldn't buy the spices on the Sabbath. According to Mark, a Resurrection had not even entered their minds; they didn't even consider the stone that would be in their way. The point is that they didn't believe in the possibility of Jesus' Resurrection. They accepted his death as final—and perhaps as failure.

In Mark's view, the young man sitting there was like an Old Testament angel, a messenger from God. What the author is trying to convey is not just that the tomb was empty; rather the concentration is on how the women are to interpret that empty tomb. What does the empty tomb mean? What it means is that "Jesus has been raised up. Go, tell the disciples to meet him in Galilee." It's interesting to note that, although Peter and the disciples get special mention in this passage, it's the women who are the first ones to receive the Resurrection message. The women are silenced by the mystery. Why they said nothing, we do not know. Whatever the reason, this verse as it stands now is a strange ending to this gospel.

This strangeness must have been felt by the early Church as well. Their tradition had more to say about the Resurrection of

Jesus. Consequently, someone composed these final eleven verses in order to clarify their belief in the Resurrection.

The emphasis in the appearances recorded in this longer ending underlines the disbelief of the disciples. They had lost their Master, and they were sad and disappointed. This account is not flattering to the disciples, since they continue to be unbelieving until the Lord himself comes to them "at table." Jesus rebukes them for their stubbornness, much as he did throughout the gospel.

The gospel ends on a note of universalism—go to the whole world and proclaim the good news. Faith and baptism are the conditions for salvation. In other words, men of all times will have to take a stand regarding the event and message of Jesus. The signs described here are indications that the reign of God has been established. Much of this terminology is from the Old Testament, and it does not mean that these are the only signs of the reign of God.

The conclusion to this section is the Ascension which, according to this author, takes place on Easter itself. The crucified Jesus is exalted and honored by his Father. In verse 20, the author calls him "Lord," a title of supreme respect. It is this Lord who works with the disciples in their proclamation of the good news and who is present in the message they preach, particularly through the signs that accompany this proclamation.

It is on this note of proclamation that Mark began his gospel, and it is on this note that this composition ends. In between, the reader witnessed conflict, struggle, misunderstanding, joy, faith, frustration, loyalty, disbelief, passion, death, Resurrection, and Ascension. The final proclamation and all that went before it—every episode, every story, every event—in some way or other described what Mark meant in chapter 1, verse 15: "This is the time of fulfillment. The reign of God is at hand! Reform your lives and believe in the gospel!"

## SOME BACKGROUND NOTES

Any way a person looks at it, the claim that Jesus rose from the dead is crucial to Christianity. Without it, we would have a dead Jesus and disbelieving, confused, frightened, and frustrated disciples. With it, we have the culmination of the gospel of Mark, the final victory in the continuous struggle presented by the author. With it, we have a living Jesus and dedicated, committed, faithful, and confident disciples. With it, we have a major ingredient in the formation of the early Christian community. Without it, we would have fraud, deceit, lying, and/or emotional instability, hallucinations, and "visions" by disturbed people. Without it, we would have either a gigantic, planned hoax engendered by the followers of Jesus, or we would be dealing with an early Church all of the members of which are crazy. In any case, the Resurrection, and the meaning of the Resurrection, is crucial to Christianity.

Christianity, of course, insists on the fact of the Resurrection. The empty tomb made a difference to the first followers of Jesus; they did not ignore that Easter event. The proclamation of the death, Resurrection, and Ascension of Jesus was the core of their preaching and the basis of their motivation.

The biblical evidence for these astounding events is confusing. The Passion narrative is precise and detailed, and the four gospel writers generally agree in their description of the death of Jesus. But the Resurrection and Ascension accounts vary greatly. One explanation for this seeming lack of agreement among the four evangelists takes us back to the conditions and problems the early Church had to face. For them a major difficulty in preaching about Jesus was to convince the listeners that Jesus was not a common criminal. After all, a listener could reason, Jesus was crucified—his was the fate of criminals. The first preachers had to demonstrate the innocence of the man crucified. Though he died like a criminal, he was not a criminal. As a result, they developed the long Passion narrative very early in the life of the Church in order to meet the objections of possible converts to Christianity. The tradition about the death of Jesus became established in a relatively set form even before the evangelists composed their gospels.

But when it came to the event of the Resurrection these early preachers did not meet the same kind of reaction. This is not to say that everyone immediately believed in the Resurrection; it is simply to say that there was no need to develop the same precision in the telling of the event. They had to "prove" that Jesus was not a criminal. They could only state that Jesus was risen from the dead: The tomb was empty, and they saw him after he had risen. Descriptions of who had seen him first under what conditions, or of how the tomb became empty are not the main points at all. The authors felt free to arrange those descriptions according to their own theological and literary purposes. The important points were to proclaim the empty tomb and to insist that it was really Jesus who was seen. Once those themes are clarified, the listener or reader could either believe or disbelieve.

There are many theories which attempt to organize and explain the various accounts of the appearances of Jesus after the Resurrection. While these theories can give us insights into what probably happened during that time, there is no one explanation that is acceptable to everyone. Did Jesus first appear to Peter in Galilee, then to the other disciples later in Jerusalem? Or were all the appearances made in Jerusalem? When did they take place? Who was there? Was there just one appearance, told by witnesses who varied the details? Or were there many appearances? These and similar questions are still being discussed by Scripture scholars. It seems unlikely that these issues will be resolved in the near future. Perhaps they may never be completely settled.

For our purposes here it is not necessary to describe all these problems. What is important, however, is to realize the fact that the Risen Lord appeared to a wide variety of people who insisted that they truly saw the self-same Jesus who lived among them and who died on the cross.

This testimony is strong and convincing; these witnesses are people who knew Jesus well. It is not a case of mistaken identity. Nor is it a case of hallucinations arising from some emotional disorder or an exaggerated expression of wishful thinking. These witnesses are emotionally stable, "ordinary" people. They include many different personality types representing various backgrounds, talents, interests, and styles of life. They all agree on one crucial fact: they saw and experienced Jesus resurrected from the dead, living again after dying. They do not waver in their testimony; many of them go to their deaths because of it. This belief and experience profoundly changes their lives for the better: they love more, they become more confident, caring, believing, helping people. They differ in details and forms of expression, but they never doubt the central experience. Jesus is undoubtedly risen from the dead.

There's an interesting switch in a word used in the Resurrection accounts. The earliest gospels, beginning with Mark, say very clearly that Jesus was raised up from the dead. Scripture scholars point out that this expression can be found in nineteen places in the New Testament. The idea in this earliest theology is that the Father raised Jesus from the tomb; the power of the Father is emphasized. In later traditions, particularly in the gospel of John, the concentration is upon Jesus: Jesus rose from the dead. The implication in this theology is that Jesus himself, by his own power, achieved a new resurrected life. John could say this because he developed a theology which spelled out the unity between the Father and the Son. But the first interpretation, namely that Jesus was raised up by the Father, is the understanding preferred by most Scripture scholars.

Reading through the various Resurrection episodes carefully will expose another problem. When did the Ascension take place? And what is the connection between the Ascension and the Resurrection? The view held by most people is that the Ascension occurred forty days after the Resurrection. This number forty comes from the Acts of the Apostles. But the number forty is generally a symbolic indication of time, not a literal one. Besides, Luke, the author of the Acts, in his own gospel does not refer to a forty-day time lapse between the Resurrection and the Ascension. He implies in the gospel that the Ascension took place on Easter. This is certainly the implication in Mark's gospel. It's quite legitimate, therefore, to think of the Ascension as occurring on Easter. Jesus is described as ascending "up" to heaven. This is symbolic language, and we need not think of heaven as "up." Speaking theologically, it is most probably accurate to say that Jesus, through his Resurrection, was glorified by the Father and that Jesus appeared to his disciples as already glorified. In this view, the Passion, death, Resurrection, and Ascension of Jesus are together considered one action, undergone for the salvation of all. It is one process, one movement. These four events are intimately connected; one cannot be interpreted apart from the other three. Theologically, then, the lapse of time between the Resurrection and the Ascension does not make much difference.

There are accounts of other resurrections in the gospels. Lazarus and the daughter of Jairus are two examples. But these people died again. Jesus rose to a life of never dying again. His existence then after the Resurrection is not an ordinary one. In fact, the New Testament mentions that some of his disciples did not recognize Jesus immediately. Jesus had changed; he was somehow different. And yet it was Jesus; the testimony is that they did see Jesus. There is therefore an element of change in Jesus as well as an element of continuity. The same Jesus changed in the process of Resurrection-Ascension. St. Paul says that "it is sown a physical body; it is raised a spiritual body" (1 Cor. 15:12). We really don't know what a spiritual body is, but we can appreciate what Paul is trying to say. After the Resurrection, there are differences, but it is the same person.

According to the gospel of Mark, the primary image of Jesus is not the crucified Messiah but the risen Lord. Jesus is first and foremost risen and glorified. Christians then are "Resurrection people." They are people who marvel at the mystery of life, affirming the basic goodness of life, saying "yes" to creation, bowing their spirits in humble affection to the mysterious beauty that pervades existence. They are people who join the continuing fight against those forces which hold back the advancement of man, whether it be social, economic, psychological, or philosophical. They are people who serve others, meeting the needs of the socially downcast, the economically deprived, or the unloved. They are people who pray, who prophesy, who serve. And they are people who believe that the reign of God has been established by the saving action of the life, death, and Resurrection of Jesus of Nazareth, who has guaranteed the final victory of good over evil.

## DISCUSSION TOPICS

*1) The Resurrection of Jesus is central to Christianity. Can you explain the relationship between the Resurrection and the following aspects of Christianity: each of the seven sacraments, the obligation of each Christian to serve others, the Church's mission to preach the good news to all, the need to pray, belief in life after death?*

*2) Judy Taylor, a friend of yours, dies unexpectedly. She and her husband Fred, also a friend of yours, were happily married for thirty years. What do you say to Fred when you talk to him about Judy's death? How do you express both the sadness of death and belief in the Resurrection? How should the Church, particularly in the funeral liturgy, handle this mixture of sorrow and joy?*

*3) Without being morbid, let yourself think of your own death. How do you want to die? How old do you want to be? Do you want to be alone or with others? What do you want to be your last words? What kind of funeral do you want? If you could write your own funeral homily, what would you say? What do you want on your tombstone?*

*4) Someone once said that the best way to prepare for our own death and resurrection is to recognize and accept the "little deaths" and "little resurrections" in our daily lives. These little deaths might include: hurting someone with a comment or being hurt by another's comment, the failure of children or parents to measure up to our expectations, loss of fame or wealth or honor, sin in any form, sickness, etc. How would you suggest turning these and other little deaths into little resurrections?*